VOTING AND NONVOTING

A BLAISDELL BOOK IN SOCIOLOGY

VOTING AND NONVOTING

IMPLICATIONS OF BROADCASTING RETURNS BEFORE POLLS ARE CLOSED

KURT LANG
State University of New York at Stony Brook

GLADYS ENGEL LANG
Center for Urban Education New York City

BLAISDELL PUBLISHING COMPANY
A Division of Ginn and Company
WALTHAM, MASSACHUSETTS · TORONTO · LONDON

WITHDRAWN
Shambaugh Library

JK
1968
1964
.L35
X
324.24
L253

IN MEMORY OF
GERT DEGENKOLBE
(1937-1964)

COPYRIGHT © 1968 BY BLAISDELL PUBLISHING COMPANY,
A DIVISION OF GINN AND COMPANY.
ALL RIGHTS RESERVED. NO PART OF THE MATERIAL COVERED BY
THIS COPYRIGHT MAY BE PRODUCED IN ANY FORM OR BY ANY
MEANS OF REPRODUCTION.
LIBRARY OF CONGRESS CATALOG CARD NUMBER: 68-19529
PRINTED IN THE UNITED STATES OF AMERICA.

Introduction: The Problem of Policy-Oriented Research

On and after election day in November 1964 we set out to investigate the effects of broadcasting early returns in areas where polls were still open. The particular focus was on the reactions of persons who had learned about the probable outcome before they had voted or could vote, and on how they felt about the practice of making predictions from an incomplete tally of votes.

In terms of mass media practices, the 1964 election centered on the quick count, just as the 1960 election dramatized the role of televised debates in the political campaign. The majority of those viewing these Great Debates believed that Kennedy had bested Nixon, that they were one of the cornerstones on which the hair-breadth Kennedy margin of victory had been built. No such significance was attributed to the early broadcasting of returns in the 1964 election. The landslide by which Johnson buried Goldwater could hardly have depended on how the election was reported on election day or on how much before poll closing time the outcome was known.

Despite the positive findings in 1960 and the negative ones in 1964, in neither instance were the issues raised by the new media practices fully resolved. Controversy over televised debates has been a campaign issue in national, state, and local contests since

1960. It should therefore have been expected that, irrespective of what the 1964 studies found, the controversy over early returns would be renewed in 1966 elections, as it was indeed, and that in all likelihood it would continue to plague networks and election officials in the future.

Any definitive findings on the existence or nonexistence of broadcast effects in 1964 were important for future policy. Prior to the election there had been considerable controversy about letting broadcast networks go on the air with their election news coverage while voting was still in progress anywhere in the country. Those for and against a ban on early broadcasts based their arguments on different principles. On the one side the news media appealed to the principle of *freedom of information* to justify a policy of no restriction. Returns, they argued, can and should be made available to *all* as soon as they are available to anyone. The right of the public to know, they insisted, could not be compromised in deference to fears expressed by candidates (or their managers) that the broadcasts might lessen their chance of being elected. The flow of information had to be kept free. If any news blackout was to be considered, it would have to be total rather than directed specifically at the election coverage by the networks. In line with this, Dr. Frank Stanton of the Columbia Broadcasting System called for a uniform voting day with polls in every locality closing at exactly the same time. This change in election practices would enable the networks to make the results from all parts of the country uniformly available to everyone.

Other persons and groups favoring curbs on the time of network broadcasts and network predictions followed a more complex, though no less compelling, line of argument: If the trend evident in the votes already counted had an effect on the decisions of those whose votes were still outstanding, as they assumed, this violated the principle of *one man and one vote.* The ballots of voters in areas where polls closed early would carry more weight; their influence would be cumulative, particularly where the size of the early majority was sufficient to determine the outcome of the election. By the same reasoning, an extra margin of effort by late voters whose man trailed by a few votes could perhaps snatch victory from a candidate who otherwise would have won.

Thus, two contending principles were invoked by those for and against curbs on these broadcasts, with the issue reduced to which value — freedom of information or voting equality — should have precedence. But the issue need not be dealt with so abstractly. Each argument rests on factual assumptions about broadcast effects that can be tested against experience. By finding out whether or not the quick dissemination of returns has any effects, and how many votes are affected and how, one can remove the discussion from the level of conjecture and give it a more solid base. In 1964 the networks declared themselves willing to use the upcoming election as a test case and to be somehow guided by the results.

We know of four studies other than our own that attempted in some way to collect data on whether the early returns in 1964 had any effect on the decisions of voters who had not yet gone to cast their own ballots. As far as we have been able to learn, four of these five studies derived at least a share of their financial support from one of the news media, whose hope it evidently was to lay to rest, once and for all, a thorny policy issue.

All five studies agreed on one general observation: the number of vote *changes* among voters who heard election returns before voting was not very large. The clarity of this finding does not, however, make it less risky to generalize about the possible effects of similar broadcasts in other elections. Had researchers found significant effects, additional research might still have been needed to identify the conditions under which such effects were most likely to re-occur. But drawing the correct inferences from negative findings is even more difficult. A failure to locate a politically significant number of vote changes in 1964 does not mean that more such changes cannot occur under different circumstances. No two elections are exactly alike.

We therefore find ourselves unable to go along with the claim of a Western broadcaster, made in a 1967 letter to *The New York Times,* that the "Lang study" (as well as others) laid to rest once and for all the idea that early returns sway late votes. The "facts" of 1964 do not suffice to refute the nagging suspicion that the broadcasting of returns before polls close might sometimes cause an election upset. No one will ever know what the outcome would have been if the election results in 1964 had followed the pattern of the Kennedy-Nixon contest four years earlier, where shifts by a minuscule percentage of the vote in several key states, including California, would have resulted in the election of Nixon. A study of the 1964 elections must take explicit account of the special circumstances of that election. Only when this is done can the results provide a point of departure for predicting what can be expected in future elections and over the long run. This, it seems to us, is the proper focus of policy-oriented research. The results should be read with this idea in mind.

Much policy-oriented social research defines its problem in particularistic terms. Because the sponsor desires quick and definitive answers, the applicability of the findings is usually time-bound. If policy-oriented social research does not always enjoy the high repute it should as an instrument of social criticism, it is not so much because findings are not valid or useful, but because the investigator has limited his function to that of a technician gathering "tactical intelligence." Too often the researcher accepts the dimensions of the problem as they are defined for him and avoids pursuing its broader implications.

Thus, findings that the 1964 election broadcasts had no net effect *on the outcome* of the election can be misread to mean that they had no effects whatsoever. In our study we have focused on a whole range of viewer reactions, including those on the covert and attitudinal level, in an effort to be analytic rather than to simply gather information. Voters did react to returns, even if they did not change their votes. By examining their reactions and the factors that seemed to influence these reactions, we sought a basis for making inferences about what might happen in future elections and for identifying possible trends.

Let us just point to some of the questions about broadcasting early returns with which our study was designed to deal. The measurement of net effect on vote totals was never our goal, though, clearly, this is what broadcasters, journalists, and other concerned parties were looking for. A study designed for that purpose could only have confirmed what every student of mass communications and of political behavior already knew from past research, namely that political communications in the closing phases of an electoral campaign sway very few people. For this and other reasons specifically related to the 1964 election, behavior changes in direct response to broadcasts heard in the last few hours of the campaign were expected to be very, very few and far between.

We were interested in locating persons who had changed their vote upon hearing early returns, but the important thing was to account for the few changes that might occur while the overwhelming majority of late voters remained "uninfluenced." Consequently we concentrated on the whole pattern of relationships among interest in the election, partisanship, political predispositions, communication exposure, and so forth as they relate to stability in vote intentions. Interest, partisanship, and political perceptions were assumed to have some influence on the likelihood that a person would hear returns before voting and, if he did hear returns, on his reactions to them. Those characteristics that increased the likelihood of exposure were also likely to minimize the likelihood of change as a direct response. Where exceptions occurred, the problem was to account for them.

Most voters, as expected, carried through on previous vote intentions. This being the case, we concentrated in our analysis on attitudinal reactions to the broadcasts. These reactions have no influence on the net effect of the broadcasts, judged by voting, but they offer clues about the psychological processes whereby stability in vote intention is maintained. The explanation of why there is no (or so little) behavioral change strikes us as equally important as the explanation of changes that do occur. Insofar as there were special circumstances that helped explain the small number of changes in 1964, we tried to use these attitudinal reactions to predict the kinds of election in which the potential for change would be maximized.

Direct effects — or the lack of them — do not exhaust the whole range of effects attributable to communications. Maintaining stability in the face of influences toward change involves some kind of adjustment, and communication research has gradually learned to include these other effects within its range of interest. For instance, deliberate nonexposure to broadcasts by persons who seek to avoid being influenced may be an irrelevant side effect for the investigator concerned only with changes in vote decisions; yet the way people come to feel about these broadcasts over the long run may have something to do with the way people come to look at voting. In that event, will the outcome of an election come, for example, to be interpreted in increasingly fatalistic terms?

Our study was also concerned with locating possible long-range and ancillary effects. For instance, we used reactions of voters to the 1964 returns as a basis for probing into the significance they attach to their balloting, into *why* people vote. Over the long run the political ramifications of early returns will depend on how they effect such motivations. The belief that large numbers of voters out West could be dissuaded from casting a ballot rests on a specific assumption: the "utility" of the ballot — its capacity to bring about a desired outcome — is what keeps voters going to the polls. Data collected in the study permitted a limited test of this assumption. It became evident that the considerations that enter into voting are considerably more complex. How else would one explain the enthusiasm with which many people cast their ballots in totalitarian countries where they have but one party slate to ratify?

The contribution of social research to policy is not exhausted by competence in collecting data and caution in their interpretation. Often the social scientist, in insisting on the ethically neutral character of his profession, defines his responsibility in purely technical terms. He directs his energies toward refining his methods of observation, increasing the accuracy with which observations are recorded, subjecting the inferences he draws to tests of reliability, and hedging whatever conclusions he draws with constant references to the many sources of possible contamination and error. By his inconclusiveness he tends to weaken the effectiveness of social science as an instrument of social criticism. The role research plays in policy decisions is consequently limited. Few issues are indeed so simple that one can obtain a clear answer from a single research project about the course policy should take.

Still, if the concept of an objective and value-free social science has any real meaning, it is to be found in the impetus given to turning every premise of custom, law, social policy, and what passes as "conventional wisdom" into an appropriate object for dispassionate scrutiny, no matter how inconvenient the findings or how offensive such skepticism may prove. This skepticism encompasses the terms in which policymakers cast a problem. Hence, we insist that a policy decision on election broadcasts should not depend on whether or not they are found to have effects on any specific election outcome. A better understanding of the nature of electoral participation and of the factors that influence it can improve the basis for reaching any tentative decision, even if it cannot settle once and for all the issue of whether restrictions on the election coverage by the networks are justified or not.

Among the contributions of this research is, first, the demonstration that the impact of network election coverage cannot be isolated from the impact of other sources of available information, especially pre-election polls and forecasts, including bulletins, rumor, and so forth. The study further suggests that suspicion will follow every close election where early returns are widely available to a large segment of the electorate before they vote. Finally, it implies that the matter of regulating the dissemination of returns on election day should be debated less in terms of the number of votes affected than in terms of the impact on the legitimacy of the electoral process.

There is much merit in the argument that incautious projections before polls close can influence the result of some elections and that therefore broadcasts should be banned to eradicate this risk. Some risk exists even when news personnel live up to the highest standards of responsibility. But there is also merit in the contrary argument, namely, that the election news provided by network coverage is more accurate than the trickle of information that would filter through to the electorate were such coverage to be banned until polls in every state had closed. The proposal for a uniform twenty-four-hour voting day — at the end of which counting everywhere would begin — seems to offer a viable way out of the dilemma. However, the question of voting and nonvoting effects in response to pre-election polls would still constitute a real issue. Perhaps the main conclusion to be drawn is that election day broadcasts are only a very minor influence on political motivation. More attention must be given to a variety of measures for improving the effectiveness of the electoral process. This study could be a catalyst for more searching debate and further inquiry into the problem.

Special acknowledgment is due to the Columbia Broadcasting System for the generous terms of contract that supported the research but permitted us to publish the findings without regard for whether or not they would bear out the policies that corporation was advocating. The study also benefitted from CBS in ways other than financial assistance. Dr. Joseph T. Klapper, director of the CBS Bureau of Social Research, and Mr. Joseph J. M. Saleh, formerly with CBS, now with Columbia Pictures, were most generous with their time and criticism, given at the expense of other pressing commitments.

The interviews in California were obtained by members of the staff of the Survey Research Center of the University of California in Berkeley under the directorship of Professor Charles Y. Glock; those in Ohio, through Special Surveys Co., Cleveland, under the directorship of Frank J. Chokel. Particular thanks are due to Professors Eugene Uyeki and Frank J. Cliffe of Case Institute of Technology for helping draw the Cleveland sample and for other assistance there. Dr. Irving Crespi of the Gallup Organization, Inc. read and carefully criticized the entire manuscript before the last draft. This naturally entitles him to a share of credit for whatever merit the final product may have and still permits him to dissociate himself from its deficiencies.

No research project of this magnitude can be completed without the services of countless individuals, the unsung footsoldiers of research. Perhaps some day there will be a plaque for them in the hall of social science, because the quality of the final report rests to a not inconsiderable degree on the willingness with which they apply themselves conscientiously to the various chores that have to be performed. Among them, the contributions of

Mrs. Shirley Hoffmann and Mr. Richard Rosen to the coding operations nevertheless call for individual recognition. No less is due to Mrs. Grace Cali McClellan and to Mr. Roland Maheu at the Center for Urban Education, and to Mrs. Veronica Abjornsen and Mrs. Sally Schirmer at the State University of New York at Stony Brook for producing a typed manuscript, in what must have been a labor of love, from only partly legible copy.

G. E. L.
K. L.

Contents

VOTING AND NONVOTING

1

The Study of Broadcast Effects

How do voters react when significant election returns are available before they have voted? The problem was forcefully brought to general attention in the presidential election of 1964. Explicit projections of a Johnson victory by the three major networks came at 3:48 P.M., at 4:43 P.M., and at 4:50 P.M. California time, long before polls in that state and neighboring states had closed, and while voting was still in progress. To the politically sophisticated spectator, the trend would have been unmistakable without such projections. Reports of Johnson's decisive sweep of populous Eastern states, and of hitherto Republican strongholds in Ohio, Indiana, and eastern Kentucky, came only minutes after polls there closed at 3:30 P.M. California time, making a national landslide a foregone conclusion. By the time many late voters out West went to the polls, the only point still at issue was the size of the Democratic sweep and the number of Republicans to be dragged down to defeat along with Goldwater.

The question raised by the coverage of the 1964 election and, for that matter, of a few earlier elections has practical and theoretical implications that extend beyond the particular election. Johnson's advantage in the East was so great that he clearly did not need the Western vote to be elected. From a practical point of view, the outcome nationally could not, even by the wildest stretching of the imagination, be attributed to the early dissemination of these returns.[1] Neither could the outcome in the many states in which, one after the other, Johnson was piling up top-heavy majorities. Yet in a close election, such as the Kennedy-Nixon contest four years previously, a shift of only a minuscule proportion of the total vote could well spell the difference between victory and defeat. Furthermore, it is conceivable that the results of several closely contested state and local races held at the same time as the Johnson-Goldwater election could have been overturned by a rather small proportion of the electorate, had they indeed been dissuaded from voting because they saw the main race as already decided. Without proof that this was what had actually happened in California, Pierre Salinger, immediately after his narrow defeat in the senatorial contest, called the electronic computer projections a "tremendous mistake," as a result of which he was "destined for defeat." [2]

Every loser, especially when the vote is close, seems to seek ready-made explanations for his defeat. The credence any charge will enjoy depends on certain propositions that, having become part of the political folklore, are their own proof. That the various propositions often contradict each other merely contributes to their usefulness; one can almost always be found to fit the specific occasion. With respect to the early broadcast of significant returns, the folklore posits at least three different effects, each of which can be invoked to explain a variety of outcomes. Thus, the clear indication of a winner is assumed to:

---

[1] A report by the Survey Research Center, The University of Michigan, concludes that "a maximum limiting effect on the turnout of Johnson supporters, coupled with a maximum positive effect on Goldwater supporters, would have been insufficient to overcome the Johnson margin that had been established by 7 P.M. EST." (mimeo).

[2] San Francisco *Chronicle*, November 4, 1964. The concern of candidates over forecasting and early returns is expressed by Walter M. Pierce, "Climbing on the Bandwagon," *Public Opinion Quarterly*, Vol. 40 (June 1940), pp. 241–43. He attributes Wilson's loss of Oregon to an afternoon news story in the *Oregon Journal* that Hughes had been elected. According to Pierce, "thousands [of Wilson supporters] did not vote at all; others switched their vote to Hughes" (p. 242).

(1) gain the forerunner additional votes and take away support from his opponent (*bandwagon effect*);

(2) bring forth a sympathy vote and extra effort to offset the handicap of the man behind (*underdog effect*); and

(3) dissuade supporters for either candidate from voting because the effort no longer seems worth while (*slack*).

Whether any of these effects best describes what happens need not be left to popular belief, but can be put to empirical test.

The Nature of Effects

The special circumstances of the 1964 election offered an excellent opportunity for observing the various responses of voters and nonvoters to significant election news, including the declaration of a winner by the networks. Differences in time zones, the late closing of polling places in some Western states, the early start of continuous election coverage by the three major networks, and the extensive use of voting machines and electronic tabulation equipment gave many members of the electorate, sometimes hours before they voted or could have voted, a clear indication of the massive Johnson majorities, which Goldwater stood absolutely no chance of overturning. Thus in the East Bay area of California, where this study of broadcast effects was conducted, polls closed at 8:00 P.M. local time, some four and a half hours later than in some Eastern states. Voters in this area could have followed the broadcasts of election returns for a full four hours before making their irrevocable vote decision. A significant proportion did in fact hear early returns and then voted.

The primary research objective of this study was to explore the factors that underlay any observed effect or lack of effect. Our point of departure was not the specific election — i.e. which of the two presidential candidates might gain or lose more, or which local contests might be influenced by the returns, but rather what had already been found out about the function of political communications during an electoral campaign. One of the most generally valid conclusions from past studies, applicable to this case, is that the closer election day approaches, the more attitudes and vote intentions will crystallize. Usually the majority of people have made up their minds by the time the parties have nominated candidates and launched campaigns. The predominant effect of campaigning being the reinforcement of prior dispositions and convictions, it follows that in the weeks before the election is held, vote switches will be the exception rather than the rule. On election day, when the returns begin to come in, few members of the electorate are still open to influence.[3]

The whole relationship between the broadcasts and the reactions of voters conforms to what can be called the "law of minimal consequences."[4] In essence this law holds that the short-run conversion potential of the media content is progressively reduced by the presence, within the communication situation, of a host of intervening conditions, each one of which tends by and large to minimize the likelihood of a response disjunctive with prior inclinations.[5] Our attention is thus drawn to the size of the group potentially open to influence, limited as it is to persons who actually hear, or hear about, election returns while still able to make a vote decision. Even within this group, the actual impact is further reduced by the normal tendency of most persons to evaluate returns they hear in the light of what each expects, what he wants to believe, and how he feels about the desirability of any particular outcome.

Very few of the effects of mass communication are immediate and direct; most are cumulative in that they usually involve prior exposure to other communications that set a framework within which any specific item of information is perceived. Thus, published poll results, political commentary, and prog-

---

[3] For a summary of findings from some relevant voting studies, see Kurt Lang and Gladys Engel Lang, "The Mass Media and Voting," in Bernard Berelson and Morris Janowitz (eds.), *Reader in Public Opinion and Communication*, Revised Edition (New York: The Free Press of Glencoe, 1965), pp. 455–72.

[4] The term was suggested by Hope L. Klapper.

[5] For a fuller statement, see Joseph T. Klapper, *The Effects of Mass Communication* (New York: The Free Press of Glencoe, 1960).

nostications of all kinds provided significant communications from which politically discerning persons could have concluded, even before election day, that Johnson would most probably win and very possibly by a landslide. Had there been any significant bandwagon effect in favor of Johnson, or an underdog effect in favor of Goldwater, it would already have had its impact on vote intentions before election day. For the vast majority of voters, returns heard before voting merely confirmed what they already believed would happen. Vote intentions, based on a picture of reality with which most voters had had ample opportunity to come to terms during the pre-election campaign, could not readily be changed by information that only served to confirm it.

The law of minimal consequences also holds for the choice between voting and nonvoting. To be able to vote, as almost everyone knows, a person must meet certain eligibility requirements and register within the district where he resides. Registration in most localities ends about four weeks before election, and failure to register is the most important factor in nonvoting. Persons not registered cannot vote, no matter how strongly events on election day may incline them toward voting.

More than that, the act of registration is, in effect, a declaration of a person's intent to vote. The overwhelming majority of those who register do indeed cast ballots. We believe that participation in a presidential election is something more than the exercise of a partisan choice; it also contains elements symbolic of a commitment to the democratic process. If this is so, the intention to vote would be highly resistant to change. A registered voter could find many instrumental justifications with regard to the importance of voting, even after an election for president is clearly "over." He could, for example, use the ballot to indicate continued faith in the man who is losing, or as a protest vote to hold down the size of the majority or to express the clearest possible repudiation of an opponent's philosophy. The wish to influence local races held concurrently with the presidential election provides still another possible motive for voting. Finally, some votes in the West may be sustained by the wish on the part of voters to show that their state's voting strength is not to be ignored and that, the Eastern results not withstanding, Westerners are bent on showing how they feel. The possibility that some votes are cast in anger should not be discounted.

Nor should one overlook the many pre-election communications specifically aimed at voters to alert them to the possible effects of the early returns and thereby to elicit reactions designed to forestall them. Salinger in a press conference the night before the election publicly expressed his concern that an early announcement of the Johnson victory might cause thousands of Californians to forgo voting and, by implication, cause Salinger to lose the election.[6] Not to be outdone, Republican National Chairman Dean Burch also directed a last-minute public appeal to network heads that they not make any projections from the early vote until polls everywhere had closed. Senator Goldwater, Burch warned, "should not be subjected to biased analysis from Democratic TV pollsters on election day."[7] According to the scuttlebutt, word had gone out to loyal Republicans urging them to vote early and so avoid being misled by projections allegedly intended to deceive and discourage them.

All the above-mentioned factors would tend to reduce the direct impact of the early election coverage. Yet the repeated use of the fast count and of computerized projections that permit the announcement of a winner with the least possible lag in time can have cumulative effects not directly related to individual vote decisions. Candidates may increasingly gear their campaigns to such projections, while voters may adopt an attitude of distrust that extends to the handling of the returns by news media. We refer in particular to the traditional significance of election night, which comes after the campaign is over and the heat generated in its course begins to abate. Especially since the advent of radio, following the count to see a winner emerge has been a memorable event, regardless of who won. When the objectivity and the presumed effects of the coverage itself become major campaign issues, election night could cease

---

[6] Oakland *Tribune*, November 3, 1964.

[7] AP story in the San Francisco *Chronicle*, November 6, 1964.

to be the unifying experience it has proved in the past in providing participation in the vote count, albeit vicariously, to all people throughout the nation at the same time.

Data from one election cannot, of course, document all the cumulative effects that might conceivably occur; nor will we attempt to do this. Even an attempt confined to pinpointing the influence of the 1964 election broadcasts on voting encounters a number of difficulties. The first of these concerns the precise magnitude of any effect among an aggregate of voters, such as the entire electorate or the electorate within any particular constituency. Does knowledge of significant returns result in an excess of changes favoring one or the other candidate? Do these changes narrow, or widen, the margin of victory, or conceivably overturn the outcome? Such questions can only be answered by studying a representative sample of voters in order to gauge from their behavior the *net effect* of the changes in opposite directions. Since the amount of change in either direction is not expected to be very large, a rather sensitive instrument of measurement is required.

Another question is what constitutes a change from a prior vote intention. A change on the overt level of behavior can mean either a switch from a previously firm intention or a vote crystallization by a person who previously has been in doubt or planned not to vote at all. Switches and crystallizations that favor the apparent winner account for bandwagon effects, those that favor the apparent loser, for underdog effects. These effects are of the direct variety; persons who are dissuaded from voting account for *indirect* bandwagon and underdog effects, depending again on which candidate suffers the loss of a vote. The number and the types of voters that actually deviate in their final vote from intentions they had before hearing returns represent the *turnover,* a phenomenon that can be studied independently of its quantitative impact on the outcome of a particular election. Such a study requires above all accurate information on how persons who appear to change would have voted had there been no early returns, and on how they actually did vote.

Furthermore, hearing returns before making a vote decision

can elicit a variety of responses, often of a subtle nature — a change in the intensity of an intention or other attitudinal reactions on the covert level — which, if carried further or under different circumstances, might lead to some form of turnover. How do voters respond upon hearing returns, especially when a winner is clearly indicated? Do they discount the information, or, if they do not, do they become more eager or less eager to go through with their previous vote intention? These and other direct responses are revealed primarily by what voters themselves are able to recount of how they interpreted, felt about, and reacted to the returns.

Because the relationship between communication (network election returns) and the response (voting behavior) is fairly complex, one has to explore a wide variety of effects, including attitudinal responses, in order to grasp the full range of possible implications that the quick dissemination of election returns may have. Although our study probably does, by indirection, cast some light on the net effect of these returns, at no time was our research design governed by the goal of making a precise quantitative estimate or a projection of the total number of votes either candidate may have lost or gained in the West because of early returns. What we sought to document in the greatest possible detail was how a variety of voters and nonvoters perceived the broadcasts and how they believed themselves to have been affected. The effects they report refer, on the overt level, to turnover and, on the covert level, to more subtle shifts of attitude.

The Research Strategy

What constitutes the most valid source of data for studying the effect of early returns? One can of course argue that the votes counted are the only payoff in an election and that, therefore, an analysis of official election statistics, or of a representative sample whose responses can be checked against these statistics, holds the greatest promise.

Against this view, we advance the following considerations: The use of election statistics depends principally upon comparisons between those voting early in the day and those voting after broadcasts can be heard. Early voters differ from late voters in numerous ways related to their voting behavior. They also differ from state to state and from locality to locality. To attribute to the election returns any of the various differences that may turn up between early and late voters is therefore totally unjustified. Also, before one can justifiably infer the influence of the early election coverage from a comparison of the vote in the Western areas with that in the East (the slightly lighter vote in the West, for instance), one must first take into account what the pattern of voting would have been without the broadcasts. This reservation holds even if we succeeded in documenting the exposure of late voters and nonvoters in the West to early returns. The populations to be compared would first have to be matched for the many characteristics known to be related to voting habits and to interest in election news. The control of the various factors by some multivariate analysis would require a large and prohibitively costly sample, and after such an analysis, the variance attributable to nonmedia factors would, in all likelihood, exceed by far any residual effect traceable to the early election returns.

We therefore restricted ourselves to interviewing "late voters," a group we defined as all those on precinct registration lists who had *not* voted by 4:00 P.M. local time, whether or not they voted later on. These registered voters were the only ones who had an opportunity to hear significant returns before voting (or before poll-closing time) and could have been influenced by what they heard. Yet this decision to concentrate exclusively on late voters, as just defined, carried with it another, far more difficult decision: to gauge impact from an after-only study instead of from a before-and-after design.

Both the before-and-after panel and the after-only study have their advantages and pitfalls. In the panel design, the same persons who have been interviewed before the election are again questioned after the election. Discrepancies between intention and self-reports of behavior can then be related to what returns a person heard before voting; they are not influenced by the respondent's recollection of how he originally intended to vote – a recollection that may be faulty.

This very considerable advantage has to be weighed against several drawbacks. To begin with, we had no foolproof way of determining in advance who among a sample would vote early (and therefore not be open to influence), who would vote late, and who would not vote at all. A pre-interview held as near election day as possible, in order to reduce the chance of events other than election-day news accounting for turnover, might have alerted the respondent; his post-election report about the returns could have been affected if we had asked him about the time he planned to vote.

We also had doubts about the meaning of a vote intention expressed the day before the election by a respondent who did not really care and did not seriously plan to vote. This was a matter of some concern, because any post-election response inconsistent with what had been said in the pre-election interview would be interpreted as turnover. In particular, we suspected that persons with low interest in the outcome, to whom the election made little difference, would be most prone to give invalid reports of how, and whether, they had previously intended to vote. Also, if they had voted but lacked firm convictions, they would be more inclined to modify their subsequent reports of how they had voted because of their knowledge of who actually won. These low-interest voters would also be the ones most susceptible to influence from early returns heard before voting, but we would never have been able to ascertain how much of the turnover we recorded represented an actual change in behavior, and how much of it was spurious and a consequence of certain unreliabilities of the panel method. In this study, where the magnitude of any effect was expected to be small, such errors could result in serious distortions. Broad generalizations might then be based on a rather high proportion of spurious effects.[8] Despite the reliance in the panel design on a direct measure of change, the observations still consist of a respondent's own account of how he feels or acts at some point

---

[8] Eleanor E. Maccoby, "Pitfalls in the Analysis of Panel Data: A Research Note," *The American Journal of Sociology*, Vol. 61:4 (January 1956), pp. 359–62.

in time. If either of the two accounts is deliberately or inadvertently distorted, much analytic effort can go into explaining causes of turnover that exists only as an effect of the method.

The after-only design we employed also relies on the respondent's own account, in this instance on a single *retrospective* account, covering both his pre-election intentions and his election-day behavior. The obvious drawback of the retrospective design is that respondents are apt to remember what they want to remember and to reconstruct events in their minds as they would like them to have occurred. Yet we believe that the sequencing and wording of questions on our interview guide at least minimized deliberate distortion. Thus, we began by asking the respondent to speak rather freely about how he had spent election night, as well as when and for how long he had been following the broadcasts of returns. Only after we had obtained this information and information on voting behavior did we begin zeroing in on the possibility of an effect. Our interviewing, moreover, began the day after the election, when recollections must still have been vivid and the respondents consequently eager to talk about and exchange their experiences. Interviewing was substantially completed within a week, with only a few cases remaining to be contacted.

We furthermore assumed that if a respondent had had a strong reaction to early returns, he would clearly remember, since the experience was recent, and be willing to reveal what it had been. Only one individual gave an unambiguous account of how he had changed his behavior, having been dissuaded from voting by what he heard about the returns. Several voters reported that on election day they had resolved prior doubts about whether to vote for a particular candidate or whether to vote at all. We do not know whether these same persons, had they been asked about their intent the day before the election, would have called themselves "undecided" or "leaning" — just as in a panel study one cannot be sure that the person who claims he is undecided is not simply resisting further probes. Whatever the reason, our method, while it gained admission of decisions made on election day, did not gain an admission from a single individual either that he had switched his vote or that he was able to resolve prior doubts about his vote for president because of any early returns he may have heard.[9] To the extent that our basic assumption may have been wrong, we did perhaps underestimate the amount of change. We doubt this, for reasons that will become clear from the data; but, in any event, there is little likelihood that we overestimated the turnover.

As a partial check on the validity of responses, we also interviewed late voters in Cuyahoga County (Greater Cleveland), Ohio. This sample, like the one in California, also consisted of persons on the registration lists who had failed to vote by 4:00 P.M. local time. The reactions of the Ohio sample provide us with a rough estimate of the proportion of possible broadcast effects in California attributable to news of very early returns from remote hamlets, local news broadcasts, and a variety of speculations and appeals available before the onset of the continuous election coverage by the networks, and also of the proportion of Californians who, even without having heard network returns, might falsely claim having been influenced.

The unique suitability of Ohio as a comparison state must be noted. Ohio, like California, had been thought a critical state, one of several with a large chunk of electoral votes that Goldwater needed to win if he were to win nationally. Both Ohio and California had highly publicized senatorial contests, judged to be very close. As it turned out, the returns from Ohio and

---

[9] The previously-cited report by the Survey Research Center found that 9 per cent of a national sample of about 1,400 reported election day behavior inconsistent with pre-election statements of intentions of several weeks before, but found no evidence that exposure to predictions was associated with changes from pre-election intentions (*op. cit.*). Perhaps more closely comparable to our own data is Harold Mendelsohn's identification of fourteen persons (out of a California sample of 1,689 voters) who reported having voted contrary to their intention as stated the day before the election. Of an additional fifty people who on the day before had called themselves undecided, only fourteen had seen or heard broadcast election returns *and* were willing to reveal how they had voted. (See H. Mendelsohn, "Exposure to Election Broadcasts and Terminal Vote Decisions," *Public Opinion Quarterly*, Vol. 30, No. 2 (Summer 1966), pp. 212–25). Finally, a preliminary report of his study of 1,736 voters in Oregon, released by John A. Rademaker, states that nineteen (or about 1 per cent) reported that what they heard "caused them to change their vote."

Indiana, coming right after the polls in these states had closed, provided the first clear signs of a decisive Democratic victory. Since the polls in Ohio closed at 6:30 P.M. EST, a full half-hour before the start of the network election coverage, the late voters in Ohio could not have been exposed to voting returns while they still had time to make a vote decision. The Ohio sample, as we shall see, also helped alert us to any sort of political pecularities that characterized late voters and nonvoters, quite apart from whether they did or did not hear election returns.

In line with our stated objective, which was to find out what types of voters would be most prone to some particular response and what conditions might maximize such inclinations, we decided on a fairly lengthy interview, with a limited sample, to provide data sufficiently rich in detail to infer the attitudinal and intellective processes underlying these responses. The average interview lasted about forty minutes. A longer interview would have been at the expense of the sample size, and any further reduction would have reduced further the number of meaningful cross-tabulations of the data that could be made.

The 364 registered voters interviewed in California constitute a field sample drawn from among all "late voters" on the precinct rosters of thirty-three East Bay, California, election districts. The particular area was chosen because it contained a population cluster of considerable diversity, though mostly urban, within a region where polls closed late (11:00 P.M., EST).

A voting roster, posted outside each polling place and available to anyone to inspect, made it relatively easy to compile lists of late voters and nonvoters. California law requires that election workers keep an accurate record by checking off on this list, every hour until 4:00 P.M., the names of those who have voted. All our interviewers had to do was to copy this list at 4:00 P.M., and request the names of those who had sent in absentee ballots.[10] This gave us a complete alphabetical list of

---

[10] Actually some errors are inevitable. Hence we checked sign-in rosters against claims by interviewees about when they had voted and, in the few instances of discrepancies, accepted the order in which the name appeared on this roster as the more valid indicator.

every registered voter in the precinct who had not voted by 4:00 P.M. local time. By taking every fifth name from this list, we achieved an unbiased selection of persons within these precincts who voted between 4:00 P.M. and 8:00 P.M. local time, and of registered nonvoters who were fully qualified to vote had they so chosen.

The precincts in both states were selected to include the widest possible range of voter characteristics. Because in the two East Bay counties of Alameda and Contra Costa, registered Democrats outnumbered registered Republicans and all forecasts were for an even higher Democratic vote for president, we deliberately overloaded the sample there with Republican precincts. This gave us a more equal distribution of the two-party vote for president than could have been expected from a more representative group of precincts. Using party registration figures, precincts were classified into those solidly Republican, those solidly Democratic, and those more evenly balanced ("swing" precincts). We then used random methods to draw election districts until each of three socio-economic levels (as judged by census data on median income and median years of schooling) was about equally represented among the types of precincts. Since solidly-Republican precincts usually represent the higher socio-economic levels, this requirement imposed a limit beyond which the selection of precincts by political complexion could not be skewed.

The method for selecting a sample that yielded interviews with 116 Ohio late voters was similar to that used in California, except that the large number of nonparty registrants (50 per cent compared with 4 per cent in California) forced us to use the 1960 presidential vote to better classify the precinct as Republican, Democratic, or "swing". Special care was taken to match the Ohio precincts as closely as possible to those in California in the relevant political and socio-economic characteristics. Despite our effort to match samples, however, we cannot assume that late voters in Ohio present us with a picture of how the California late vote would have gone had people known nothing about the election trends.

The Late Vote in California and Ohio

Reports of late voters on how they cast their votes show that this selection of precincts failed to yield the desired near-equal representation of supporters for the two presidential candidates. Part of the explanation lies, of course, in the large number of Republicans who in 1964 cast ballots for Johnson. The frequency of such cross-overs among normally Republican voters is indicated by the 57.7 per cent majority Johnson received in the California precincts and the 61.8 per cent majority he received in Ohio. This does not, however, explain why the undersupply of Goldwaterites in the two late-voter samples should have been greater than that in the total vote within these same precincts (Table 1.1).

Before we ask whether or not this low Goldwater vote represents an effect of the early returns, another question must be resolved: Were late voters in the two areas more strongly for Johnson than early voters, *or* is the apparent difference due to some methodological shortcoming in that Democrats were more often selected for interviews — or respondents prone to state that they had voted for Johnson even if they had not? To examine these possibilities, we looked at the party registrations of those who were drawn into our sample and compared those interviewed with those whom we failed to reach. We also compared the party registrations of voters in these precincts and the total vote for president and senator, in order to predict from the registrations in our sample what the two-party distribution of their vote for president and senator should have been. This analysis helped to explain why the expected numbers of Goldwater voters were not reached. The analysis also highlights difficulties inevitably encountered in this type of research.

To begin with, an excess of registered Democrats actually interviewed was not the result of less-than-complete sample coverage, but reflects the excess of registered Democrats in the total sample, among those interviewed and those not interviewed.

When we estimate from these party registration figures the "probable" Democratic majority among the late voters, it seems

Table 1.1 Political Composition of Precinct Registrations and of Late-Voter Samples

	PRECINCTS						INTERVIEWS					
	Registration		*Presidential Vote*		*Senate Vote*		*Registration*		*Presidential Vote*		*Senate Vote*	
CALIFORNIA	N	%	N	%	N	%	N	%	N	%	N	%
Democratic	3967	48.0	3834	57.7	3150	46.3	191	52.5	211	63.2	155	47.1
Republican	3977	48.1	2812	42.3	3649	53.7	151	41.5	123	36.8	174	52.9
Other*	323	3.9					22	6.0	(15)		(20)	
Total†	8267	100.0	6646	100.0	6799	100.0	364	100.0	334	100.0	329	100.0
Ratio D/R††	(1.00)						(1.26)					
OHIO												
Democratic	763	25.8	1507	61.8	998	42.2	40	34.5	76	79.2	44	43.1
Republican	749	25.3	931	38.2	1367	57.8	19	16.4	20	20.8	58	56.9
Other*	1443	48.9					57	49.1	(8)		(4)	
Total†	2955	100.0	2438	100.0	2365	100.0	116	100.0	96	100.0	102	100.0
Ratio D/R††	(1.02)						(2.11)					

*Nonparty and "third" party registrants—persons who refused to state how they voted.
†Precinct vote and sample votes do not include nonvoters or persons who abstained from voting for the particular office. Persons who refused to state their vote are given in parentheses.
††Democratic registrants ÷ Republican registrants.

that the disproportionately high Democratic registration just about accounts for the discrepancy from the total vote in these precincts. In California, the percentage of registered Democrats was 4.5 per cent higher among late voters than among all voters, and the corresponding vote gain by Johnson was 5.5 per cent.[11] In Ohio, the proportion of votes Johnson received from the late-voter sample exceeded that in the total precinct vote by 17.4 per cent, but the proportion of registered Democrats was larger by only 9 per cent; Republican registrations dropped, and those without a stated party affiliation remained at about the 50 per cent mark. If the relative number of Democratic and Republican registrations indicates the division of party preferences among the nonparty registrants, the heavy Johnson majority in the Ohio late vote appears once again to be fully accounted for by party registration.

There may still be some doubt as to how accurately we identified the late voter, as distinct from the nonvoter and early voter. It will be recalled that all those voting before 4:00 P.M. were automatically excluded by our method of selection. After the election we verified the identification of late voters in the sample by checking the precinct rosters, which voters had to sign in the exact order in which they voted. From the position of the respondent's signature we could estimate with reasonable accuracy the time he had gone to the polls. Eliminated from our sample was every one of the doubtful cases — e.g. the interviewee who said he had voted early even though his name had *not* been checked off the posted registration list.

Doubts about the validity of self-reports on vote decisions are somewhat more difficult to dispel: the ability to verify whether

---

[11] Other studies support our finding that the California late vote was probably more strongly for Johnson than the early vote. Mendelsohn, *op. cit.*, gives statistics from which the pre-4:30 P.M. vote can be compared with the post-4:30 P.M. vote. The proportion for Johnson was 10 percentage points higher in the late vote – 64 per cent compared with 54 per cent. This may have been due to an unusually early Goldwater vote. According to another study, the proportion of votes cast for Johnson remained fairly constant in the period after 1:00 P.M. See Douglas Fuchs, "Election-Day Radio-Television," *Public Opinion Quarterly*, Vol. 30, No. 2 (Summer 1966), p. 230.

and when a person voted does not extend to how he voted. Previous election studies have noted a tendency on the part of some voters to report falsely that they had voted for the winner, and so inflate post-election survey reports of the actual margin of victory. Had we used the panel design, these claims could have produced spurious turnover and pointed to a bandwagon effect in response to the returns, even if none had occurred. In post-election surveys using respondents' self-reports of how they voted, this bandwagon effect has been estimated at about 3 per cent.[12] This figure parallels fairly closely the number of nonvoters whose claim that they had voted was not substantiated by our check of the records. In this study, we found seven self-alleged voters whose names did not appear on the official sign-in rosters of their precincts and who, we have good reason to believe, did not cast ballots. All but one of the seven claimed that they had voted for Johnson. If this category of person contributes significantly to a post-election bandwagon effect manifest immediately after an election, this particular source of distortion was eliminated. We discarded all seven from our analysis, as most of their other responses would likewise have been invalid.

Turning to the self-reports of verified late voters, we must try to assess how persons refusing to reveal their presidential vote might affect the total picture of the late vote. The relevant figures are in the third row of Table 1.1. Refusals were somewhat more frequent among registered Republicans, presumably among those who had reservations about Goldwater and were in conflict or ambivalent about how to vote. Yet we have no way of telling whether a refusal by a Republican was meant to conceal a vote for Goldwater over which he had many misgivings, or whether he had defected from the Republican party and by voting for Johnson had contributed to its defeat. The point is that the absolute number of refusals is not large enough to alter the general picture, even if every one in this group had

---

[12] Angus Campbell *et al.*, *The American Voter* (New York: John Wiley & Sons, 1960), p. 75.

voted for Goldwater. They were excluded from any analysis relating reactions to presidential preferences, or from any attempt to surmise the impact of the returns on the actual vote.

When we compare the self-reports of late voters on how they voted for president with those on how they voted for senator, we note a rather different pattern of deviation of the late vote from the total vote. In neither state do the ballots cast for senator reflect the clear majorities of Democratic registrants among late voters. Yet in relation to the total vote, the late vote for senator was slightly more Democratic in California, where the Democrat lost, than it was in Ohio, where he finally won by the narrowest margin. The Senate vote in both states was extremely close. The Murphy-Salinger contest was not decided until well after midnight, and the Taft-Young race was a "cliff-hanger" with the final declaration of the winner delayed for at least another day. Neither this closeness nor the generally lower interest in Senate elections should have provided any strong incentive for interviewees to misrepresent their actual Senate vote.

If the big majorities Johnson received from late voters is a valid phenomenon, can it be traced to the influence of early election returns? Such an inference is clearly not warranted: the difference between the proportion of Johnson voters interviewed and the proportion of the total vote he received was greater by far in Ohio than in California. So is the disparity among late voters between the proportion of Democratic votes for president and the proportion of Democratic votes for senator. Despite an overwhelming majority for Johnson in the Ohio late vote, Young received only 42 per cent of this vote, while Salinger received 46 per cent among a group of voters who gave Johnson a much smaller majority. Thus, ticket splitting that favored Johnson over the Democratic senatorial candidate was greater in Ohio. Since polls in Ohio had closed before significant returns could possibly have been heard, the top-heavy Johnson majority among the late voters there evidently had no connection with election news. It probably reflects the influence of local political factors and the demographic composition of the Ohio late vote, particularly on the frequency of ticket splitting.

Perhaps these comparisons between California and Ohio, if they reveal anything at all, point to a complexity in voting patterns that no facile hypothesis can adequately explain. In attempting to understand some of the relationships involved, we have gone beyond simple "objective" indicators of change and have tried to probe subjective reactions as they were reported by voters. Except in those instances where a completed interview was discarded because of a discrepancy between the time a respondent said he had gone to the polls and what our inspection of voting rosters revealed, we have treated what people told us as honest reports of their experiences, pressing our analysis of these data to clarify as far as possible the kinds of responses to early returns and their possible effects.

In the main body of research findings, we will offer no further comparisons of the late vote with either the early or the total vote. Most comparisons are between late voters (and nonvoters) exposed to returns — network broadcasts in particular — before they made their vote decision and those not so exposed. Comparison between other subgroups in the sample are also employed whenever they help pinpoint, qualify, or clarify possible effects the early returns may have had on different types of people.

To repeat: The research design was geared to locating patterns and relationships, mostly among political preferences, political assessments, and exposure to news about the election prior to voting or prior to poll closing time. The basic independent variable is exposure, which we tried to document as carefully as possible. Accordingly, we have:

(1) an *exposed group*, namely, late voters who went to the polls after they had heard some returns and registered nonvoters who heard them before polls closed;

(2) a *no-exposure group*, namely, late voters and registered nonvoters in California who did not avail themselves of the opportunity to hear returns before voting or while they could still have voted; and

(3) a *no-opportunity group*, namely, the comparison group in Ohio, which we occasionally used to check and clarify any apparent relationship between exposure to returns and voting behavior.

•2•

Orientations to the Early Election Coverage

Voters in California, as throughout the country, approached the election broadcasts with certain expectations and preconceptions. Of special interest are those expectations and preconceptions that could affect people's reactions to returns they heard before voting.

One element of considerable significance is the background of information and comment provided by newspapers, as a result of which citizens had been alerted to possible effects of these broadcasts. To what extent had late voters in California become aware of the controversy over the early start of the broadcasts and then reacted to it on the basis of what they had read? Did they see themselves as candidates for "influence"? Did some deliberately wait for election news before they voted, or, conversely, did some deliberately not hear news in order to avoid the risk of being influenced?

Experience with past election broadcasts was another element that possibly influenced reactions. What a person looked for could have been affected by what he knew of how election returns were assembled and how predictions were made from very incomplete returns, and by how much trust he placed in them.

It is with some of these possibilities in mind that later in this chapter we also take a look at the characteristics of those in our late-voter sample who had followed network returns before voting or before polls closed, at their political orientations and their orientations to the election broadcasts. Are there indications that this group was more susceptible than the rest to influence from these broadcasts? Discussion of these and other matters in this chapter is meant to be suggestive rather than definitive. It merely sets the framework for our subsequent discussion of effects.

Newspapers on the Election Coverage

Ninety-three per cent of the sample interviewed reported being regular readers of at least one of three major local newspapers; 40 per cent said they read two or more. On the assumption that what people expected from election night broadcasts and how they felt about them was shaped in part by what they could have read in the newspapers, we examined, over a two-week period beginning Monday, October 25, and spanning the election, the content of all items in the San Francisco *Chronicle*, the San Francisco *Examiner*, and the Oakland *Tribune* in which the issue of the early election returns was taken up.

During the week before the election, the *Tribune* carried three news items, the *Chronicle*, one, and the *Examiner*, none, that dealt explicitly with these matters. Of the three items carried by the *Tribune*, two were based on UPI releases. They gave the details of the plan for a pooled coverage by the press associations and networks. This new Network Election Service was promising to have about half the California vote tallied within 90 minutes after the polls had closed.

In contrast to the factual reportage, the more controversial aspects of the speed-up in the count and the early coverage were dealt with only in columns and editorials, at least during the week before the election. For example, a person reading the *Tribune*, the Republican paper published by former Senator William F. Knowland, could also have read a column by Hal Humphreys on "Computers and Ballots," copyrighted by the Los Angeles *Times*. Humphreys was most alarmed by the definite possibility that the election might be all over before millions of Westerners had marked their ballots. He therefore called on the Western governors to push for legislation to advance the closing of the polls in their states to a time before the networks could possibly carry significant returns from the East. He took a dim view of "promises from the TV networks to keep a conservative rein on their tons of electronic computers. . . . CBS this Nov. 3 is launching what it calls a 'massive study' of voters in the West to determine if they are influenced by early election declarations. It goes without saying, therefore, that CBS intends to have an early winner spewed out of its computers. Otherwise, there would be nothing to observe in this 'massive study.'"[1]

The note sounded by television columnist Gail Wrixon was somewhat similar, though perhaps more restrained. She reported that a new system for analyzing returns had been developed to avoid a repeat of 1960, when the computers had falsely predicted a Nixon victory a short time after polls in the East closed and with only a minute fraction of the vote counted. This time, she implied, the three networks had agreed *not* to declare or predict a presidential winner until 270 electoral votes had been "won."[2]

The day before the election, Pierre Salinger, the Democratic incumbent seeking re-election to his Senate seat, took up this issue in a press conference. A brief news item, headlined "TV Could Sway Vote, Pierre Says," made the back pages of the afternoon *Tribune*, but the other two newspapers gave it considerable prominence on the morning of election day. Salinger was reported sharply critical of alleged plans to pronounce the winner as early as 4:30 P.M. California time. The thousands who might forgo voting, the senator held, would include more Democrats than Republicans. The same election morning edition of the *Chronicle* also carried the previously mentioned AP story of Dean Burch's appeal to the networks that they refrain from making "early and unwarranted interpretations" until after polls closed.

---

[1] Oakland *Tribune*, October 29, 1964.

[2] San Francisco *Chronicle*, November 1, 1964.

The point is not so much that these dire predictions came from persons with an obvious political ax to grind, but that they received so much space on election morning. The *Chronicle,* which had endorsed Johnson and Salinger, and the *Examiner,* which had endorsed Johnson and Murphy (Salinger's Republican opponent), issued their own editorial warnings against the broadcasts. Under the headline "Trigger-Happy Election Reports," the *Chronicle* on its editorial page lent backing to Salinger's suspicions. The editors voiced fears that projections might "unduly influence the election," and called for some way of keeping secret the vote count of all precincts until all polls had closed, or, failing that, for a federal law forbidding any state to begin counting until all votes had been cast. The *Examiner* carried a front-page election day editorial with a clearly nonpartisan appeal headlined "Early or Late . . . Vote!" It exhorted all readers, "Don't let TV or radio election bulletins beguile you into thinking your vote no longer matters." In its back pages columnist Dick Nolan declared himself "uneasy" because "big television [had] taken over the election. . . . In the process the whole solemn business of great national decisions is somehow cheapened." Dwight Newton, the television columnist, joined this lament, suggesting that "perhaps the only way to lick it is to vote before they turn on the machine . . . with an absentee ballot 30 days in advance." [3]

We have no way of estimating the impact of any of these stories on those who read them. Yet this brief review of press dispatches and comment makes it clear that by election day the coverage had itself become an issue. The general tone was one of alarm, and the mechanics of reporting an election were generally underplayed. After the election, however, the tenor of the press coverage changed somewhat. The *Chronicle,* its prior editorial warning against "trigger-happy election reports" notwithstanding, carried two news stories dealing with the radio and television coverage in which it emphasized the early time at which the predictions of victory had come. The broadcasts were portrayed as a race, along with the political race.

---

[3] San Francisco *Examiner,* November 3, 1964.

NBC was said to have "beat the other two" in being the first to make an explicit prediction that Johnson would win. Editorially the paper continued to sound a somewhat different note. Its editors declared themselves "more than ever convinced [that] computerized predictions on television [were a] threat to the very basis of democracy." Any voter who happened to tune in before he voted either "became discouraged by the thought that the national outcome was already determined . . . or . . . got so wrapped up in the seductive showmanship that he didn't bother to go to the polls and vote, after all." [4]

Much other comment was negative in still a different way. A UPI story in the *Tribune* praised the work of the election news pool; another in the same paper credited the early computer projection with cutting down on the usual amount of post-election-night "hangover." But Prescott Johnson, in the *Examiner*, described himself as bored. "I could hardly wait to get home. . . . By 8:02, the set had warmed up. . . . But it was too late. LBJ must have won with the first punch. I didn't see it. Anyway the fight was all over, so I finished a beer and went to bed." Among the readers who took up the issue in "Letters to the Forum" was a person who told of his great interest over the past eight years in watching the televised returns. If the networks in their next national coverage should persist with their projections, he threatened, two years hence "I am going to keep my television set off."

Past "Experience" and Attitudes Toward Predictions

Many news writers seemed to have overlooked that what was unique about the 1964 election was not so much the use of computers as the ability of the rapid coverage to make immediately clear to all who were exposed to broadcasts the one-sided nature of the presidential contest. Though computers had been used since 1952, it was in 1960, the year of the Kennedy–Nixon photo finish, that the names of these mechanical robots became household words. Shortly after the first meaningful returns came in, computers primed with data from past elections on certain bellweather precincts across the country began giving out

---

[4] San Francisco *Chronicle*, November 4, 1964.

projections about the outcome. The earliest prediction, coming at 4:15 P.M. (Pacific time), was for a Nixon victory. It had to be modified as more complete figures from large Eastern cities became available, and by 5:00 P.M. Kennedy was expected to get 51 per cent of the popular vote. By 7:00 P.M. the election must have appeared to many as pretty much decided, but through the rest of that long night and into the early morning the Kennedy victory seemed far less sure in the light of an extremely narrow popular-vote margin and the number of large states whose electoral vote was still in doubt.[5] For many of those tuned in, the reporting based on the new machines proved a test of their fallibility — or magic, to those who chose to view it as such.

Just a few months before the 1964 election, the networks gave national coverage to the Republican primary in California, in which New York's Governor Rockefeller was pitted against Goldwater. The Arizona senator had been declared the winner by CBS television on the basis of highly incomplete returns. At the time the prediction was made, Rockefeller still held a lead in the votes tallied. The hair-breadth margin of the ultimate Goldwater victory, together with the fact that the prediction came while voting was still in progress in the San Francisco Bay region, where polls closed a full hour later than in the rest of the state, stirred up much speculation and controversy. Some argued that the early and barely warranted prediction might have been responsible for the outcome, because it had discouraged from voting a large number of people in an area judged to be the main center of Rockefeller support. So recent a controversy over the use of computers could be expected to have had some impact on judgments about their infallibility and possible misuse.

To get some measure of the past "experience" of late voters, we asked them about the four previous presidential elections (1948, 1952, 1956, and 1960) and the California primary to find out if they had watched or listened to election returns from any of them for one hour or more. According to these reports, Cali-

---

[5] Theodore H. White, *The Making of the President 1960* (New York: Pocket Books, Inc., 1961). In Chapter 1, White uses Eastern Standard Time to cite the rapidity of projection.

fornia late voters, 62 per cent of whom had previously followed three or more election broadcasts, appear to have been somewhat more experienced than Ohioans, only 53 per cent of whom had previously followed this many broadcasts. Yet the greater amount of experience in California reduces itself in the main to the larger number who had followed the California primary—77 per cent in California compared with 53 per cent in Ohio. Interest in this primary would naturally have been greater among Californians, and the fact that the coverage was carried during the prime viewing hours must also have contributed to the larger audience. Unfortunately we failed to obtain any information (beyond these reports on minimal exposure) about what was remembered from the previous elections with regard to predictions or the use of computers. We did, however, obtain data from our respondents about their knowledge of how such predictions are made and on their attitudes toward computers. An examination of the relationship between a person's knowledge and attitude and his past experience permits us to make some inferences about the possible impact of these broadcasts over time.

Each person in California and Ohio was asked to indicate for each of a number of statements whether he agreed more with its content than he disagreed *or* disagreed more than he agreed. Three of these statements dealt with the use of computers in predicting election results:

> "Electronic computing machines are more often wrong than right when they pick a winner before most votes have been counted."
> "All that computers do is to count the vote very quickly."
> "Being told who the winner will be early in the evening before most votes have actually been counted takes the fun out of election night broadcasts."

The first statement is essentially a *credibility* judgment; the second is a test of *knowledge;* and the third expresses an *attitude* toward the use of computers in the reporting of returns.

Despite differences in exposure to the California primary returns, the over-all distribution of responses in the two states was

Table 2.1 Attitudes Toward Computers

Statement	*California*		*Ohio*	
Computers "wrong"	N	%	N	%
Disagree	261	72	74	64
Agree or can't say	99	27	41	35
No information	4	1	1	1
Computers "only count"				
Disagree	148	41	40	35
Can't say	20	5	14	12
Agree	193	53	62	53
No information	3	1	—	—
Computers "kill fun"				
Disagree	183	50	66	57
Agree	163	45	44	38
Can't say	17	4	5	4
No information	1	*	1	1
Total respondents	364		116	

* <.5%

basically similar (Table 2.1). Respondents in both places expressed a good deal of faith in the reliability of computerized predictions but exhibited considerable ignorance about what a computer does. Californians were somewhat more knowledgeable, more apt to trust the machines, and, whether or not for that reason, more likely to feel that knowing the results early in the evening took the fun out of following the returns.

In California, computer projections enjoyed greater credibility among experienced viewers (who had followed election broadcasts in three or more elections in the past) than among the relative novices (two or fewer), a relationship *not* replicated in the Ohio sample, where computers seemed to enjoy slightly less credibility, even among those with experience (Table 2.2). From this difference between the two areas, we infer that the California primary, held the preceding June, played a considerable part in familiarizing Californians with the predictive capabilites of these machines. The inference is confirmed by the greater credi-

Table 2.2 Credibility of Computers and Prior Exposure

	CALIFORNIA				OHIO			
*Credibility**	*Experienced Viewers††*		*Novices*		*Experienced Viewers*		*Novices*	
	N	%	N	%	N	%	N	%
High	208	75	53	65	56	64	18	64
Low	70	25	29	35	31	36	10	36
Total responses†	278	100	82	100	87	100	28	100
	Followed California Primary		*Did Not Follow*		*Followed California Primary*		*Did Not Follow*	
	N	%	N	%	N	%	N	%
High	210	76	51	62	38	62	36	67
Low	68	24	31	38	23	38	18	33
Total responses†	278	100	82	100	61	100	54	100

*High credibility = "agree"; low credibility = "disagree" or "can't say."
†Does not include respondents on whom adequate information was not obtained.
††Experienced viewers had followed in three or more elections; novices in no more than two.

bility the computer enjoyed among late voters who followed the California primary returns compared with those who did not — the difference appears only in California; no such effect was noted in Ohio.

The immediate hunch might be that the political relevance of past viewing experience, and not the actual viewing itself, had the greater influence on the credibility judgment. However, despite a good many spontaneous expressions from staunch Goldwater supporters of untempered hostility to all kinds of predictions — by polls as well as by computers — there was absolutely no difference between the credibility judgments of Democrats and Republicans, or between that of persons who had voted for Goldwater in the primary and all other late voters. Apparently these credibility judgments are less colored by political preferences than are attitudes toward the *use* of polls and computers for making predictions.[6]

[6] See Chapter 7.

By agreeing with the statement that "all computers do is to count the vote very quickly," approximately half the respondents in both states indicated that they had a false concept of how computers were used in reporting elections. More Californians than Ohioans knew the correct answer, and more of the latter were ready to acknowledge that they had no idea. Correct knowledge was likewise related to the amount of past exposure, with the more experienced viewers in both states more likely to express disagreement with the false statement of what the computer does (Table 2.3). The greatest increment in knowledge was found among Californians who had followed the primary, while in Ohio exposure to the primary appeared to have an effect in the reverse direction without this difference being in any way reliable.

"Being told who the winner will be early in the evening before most votes have actually been counted takes the fun out of

Table 2.3 Knowledge of Computers and Prior Exposure

	CALIFORNIA				OHIO			
*Knowledge**	*Experienced Viewers††*		*Novices*		*Experienced Viewers*		*Novices*	
	N	%	N	%	N	%	N	%
Correct	123	44	25	30	35	40	5	17
Don't know	13	5	7	8	6	7	8	28
Wrong	141	51	52	62	46	53	16	55
Total responses†	277	100	84	100	87	100	29	100
	Followed California Primary		*Did Not Follow*		*Followed California Primary*		*Did Not Follow*	
	N	%	N	%	N	%	N	%
Correct	121	44	27	32	19	31	21	38
Don't know	11	4	9	11	6	10	8	15
Wrong	146	52	47	57	36	59	26	47
Total responses†	278	100	83	100	61	100	55	100

*Correct = "disagree"; don't know = "can't say"; wrong = "agree."
†Does not include respondents on whom adequate information was not obtained.
††Experienced viewers had followed in three or more elections; novices in no more than two.

election night broadcasts" was the third of the statements having to do with computers. It was the one to which a few respondents objected vehemently on the grounds that these broadcasts were serious business and hardly meant to be fun. Californians, who had heard predictions earlier in the day than Ohioans, were also by and large more ready to think that the show had been spoiled by early pronouncement of who won. Such a reaction was only slightly more frequent among experienced viewers than among novices, and did not appear to be a response to the California primary (Table 2.4). There was a greater tendency by registered Republicans than Democrats to agree with the criticism implied by the statement — a suggestion, perhaps, that the reactions contained an element of satisfaction or disappointment about the outcome of the 1964 election. Republicans who had been for Rockefeller prior to Goldwater's nomination were most critical of all — 55 per cent of former Rockefeller supporters seconded the statement that computers had indeed killed their fun compared to 45 per cent of the entire California sample.

Table 2.4 Attitudes Toward Computers and Prior Exposure

	CALIFORNIA				OHIO			
Attitude	*Experienced Viewers*†		*Novices*		*Experienced Viewers*		*Novices*	
	N	%	N	%	N	%	N	%
Still fun	134	50	49	61	50	60	16	62
Kills fun	132	50	31	39	34	40	10	38
Total responses*	266	100	80	100	84	100	26	100
	Followed California Primary		*Did Not Follow*		*Followed California Primary*		*Did Not Follow*	
	N	%	N	%	N	%	N	%
Still fun	138	52	44	57	33	58	33	62
Kills fun	130	48	33	43	24	42	20	38
Total responses	268	100	77	100	57	100	53	100

*"Can't say" answers not included.

†Experienced viewers had followed in three or more elections; novices in no more than two.

Yet even with the elements of a suspense drama lacking, the more experienced viewers contributed disproportionately to the number of hardy souls in California who stuck with the election broadcasts until *after* midnight, long after the main event had been fully decided. Evidently it was not only the desire to know the outcome of the presidential race that kept the election night audience with the coverage. So, we shall look at some other elements that kept people watching.

Each respondent, regardless of whether he had followed returns in 1964, was asked: "Speaking about broadcasts of election returns in general now, this card contains five comments which people have made about how they feel about television and radio election returns. Please read these statements and tell me which *one* statement is closest to how you yourself feel about these broadcasts." The statements included an option that permitted the respondent to say that he found the returns "boring"; only about 10 per cent opted for this view. Among the five statements there was an overwhelming concentration of responses — an identical 60 per cent in each state — on "getting an idea of how people in the country feel." The "excitement of a close race" ran a poor second in both states, receiving about 15 per cent of all mentions. About 8 per cent said they wanted to see how the candidates reacted to victory and defeat, while "early prediction of the outcome" came last with about 5 per cent. A few could not — or would not — accept any of the five statements.

This question may well have elicited stock answers. It is therefore useful to compare the distribution of responses with those to another question, totally unrelated to the first, in which all those *who had followed returns at any time in 1964* were asked to select from a card the particular items "important to you personally when you selected a channel or station." Each was then asked, "Which of these things [including anything mentioned by the respondent not on the original list] was *most* important to you?"

The majority of responses in both states referred to some quality of the reporting. In each state, "commentators that I know and like" was cited by about one third of all who had followed

Shambaugh Library

returns as their most important consideration, and thus led all others by far (Table 2.5). Helpful interpretations, straight and unbiased reporting, human-interest features, and an entertaining coverage also received their share of mentions. "Fastest vote count" and "earliest prediction of the winner"—two items relating to the speed with which results would become known—together attracted less than 10 per cent of the responses.

If the demand for speedy coverage is no more widespread than implied by these responses, one can indeed question the competitive emphasis the networks give to an early prediction. A more likely interpretation is that the choices of the election night audience are made in terms of other, perhaps more peripheral, con-

Table 2.5 Considerations in Choosing a Channel or Station (per cent)

	CALIFORNIA (*N* = 347)*		OHIO (*N* = 109)*	
Items Mentioned	*All Mentions*	*Most Important*	*All Mentions*	*Most Important*
Commentators	62	31	75	35
Straight and unbiased reporting	26	12	48	21
Helpful interpretations	39	10	44	10
Entertaining coverage	25	5	40	5
Human interest	26	3	35	6
Fastest vote count	15	6	29	7
Earliest prediction	11	2	27	2
Local returns†		3		0
Reception†		7		2
Favorite station†		3		2
Advertising and things to be avoided†		1		1
Other and inadequate information		15		9
Total (per cent)		98††		100

*Persons who followed returns in 1964.
†Volunteeered by respondents without being on original list and therefore not included in tabulation of "all mentions."
††Due to rounding.

siderations only because they take for granted an up-to-date, rapid coverage; there were no substantial differences among the networks in this regard, and it was much easier to identify a network by its commentators and distinctive style of reporting. In other words, the emphasis on the other considerations does not necessarily mean inattentiveness to or a lack of concern with being informed as fast as possible.

When we examine the number of times an item was mentioned as a consideration in choosing a channel or station, regardless of whether it was the most important or merely a subsidiary element in the choice, both "fastest vote count" and "earliest prediction" receive considerably more mentions but still lag far behind "familiar and appealing commentators," which continues to occupy the top spot. There now appears also a rather considerable discrepancy between the number in California and in Ohio who mention fast coverage and early prediction, with late voters in the Eastern state emphasizing these two items about twice as often as late voters in the West.[7] Since coverage began only *after* polls had closed in Ohio, voters there would naturally be more eager to learn the outcome without having to stay up unusually late. Still, even in Ohio, speed of coverage mattered very little in comparison with other considerations. We must conclude that in California where the viewer was likely to have become fully certain of the outcome before ever settling down to an evening of following returns, a large number repudiated the concept of the fast count and, indeed, did think "computers killed the fun."

We shall now turn our attention to the question of who among the California late voters had been following returns before he himself voted or, if he did not vote, before polls closed.

Who Followed Returns Before Voting?

People, in talking about the returns, did not make too clear a distinction between the continuous network broadcasts and ear-

[7] To be sure, Ohio interviewees saw more items as important than did Californians, including the five items not related to speed of coverage, but the increase of mentions on the last two is especially noticeable.

lier news bulletins, so we constructed our own criteria for judging whether or not a person had been following network returns before voting. At the very beginning of the interview, before the issue of voting had even been raised, each respondent was asked, "At about what time did you start following the returns?" Each was also asked when he had finally turned off the set, and whether, before doing so, he had ever turned away from it for about fifteen minutes or more. This series of questions gave us a fairly complete record of the respondent's behavior with regard to the election broadcasts, from which we could then determine whether his pre-voting information was likely to have come from network broadcasts.

Approximately equal proportions of late voters voting at different times had begun following the broadcasts of returns at 4:00 P.M., the time the networks went on the air with their election coverage (Table 2.6). Among each group of voters the cumulative per cent who, at any given hour, had begun following returns jumps ahead markedly of that among people voting later. As each group votes, it catches up and then for a time moves ahead of those who have still to vote. For instance, among those voting by 5:30 P.M., only 40 per cent had begun to follow returns by 5:00 P.M.; by 6:00 P.M., 69 per cent were tuned in. The same pattern characterizes the other two groups of voters. In the group of 5:30 to 6:30 P.M. voters, the proportion who had begun following returns lagged behind that of earlier late voters, but by 7:00 P.M., the proportion was identical with that among the earlier voters. The lag is greatest among the late-late voters, but they too had caught up by 7:30 P.M. (Voting from 7:30 to 8:00 P.M. was extremely light.) It is clear that most late voters did whatever they had to do during election day and then went to vote; in many cases, as respondents revealed during the interviews, this was on the way home from work. As far as nonvoters are concerned, the proportion who had begun to follow returns at any given hour appears consistently to have lagged behind the rest, and more of them never followed returns at all.

Defined as "directly exposed to returns before voting" were only those who had followed network broadcasts for a half hour or more before the time at which they said they had cast their

Table 2.6 Cumulative Per Cent Exposed to Network Election Coverage

	Voting Time									
Began following returns . . .	After 4:00 P.M. but by 5:30 P.M.		After 5:30 P.M. but by 6:30 P.M.		After 6:30 P.M.		Nonvoters		*Total Sample*	
	N	cum. %	N	cum. %	N	cum. %	N	cum. %	N	cum. %
at 4:00 P.M.	29	20	22	18	14	18	2	17	68	19
by 5:00 P.M.	58	40	36	29	23	29	4	33	122	36
by 6:00 P.M.	99	69	70	56	39	49	5	42	214	59
by 7:00 P.M.	117	81	101	81	57	71	7	58	283	78
by 7:30 P.M.	122	85	106	85	68	85	7	58	304	84
by 8:00 P.M.	131	91	111	89	71	89	9	75	324	89
after 8:00 P.M.	138	96	120	96	78	98	9	75	347	96
Total	144	100	125	100	80	100	12	100	364	100
Followed returns before voting	40	28	50	40	47	59	7	58	146	40

ballot, or from at least 7:30 P.M. in case they had not voted at all. This excludes those who may merely have heard something from news bulletins, who relied on hearsay or newspaper headlines to give them some clue, or who may have caught a few impressions on their way to vote. According to this "objective" criterion, two out of five persons in the California sample[8] had been following returns before voting (last row of Table 2.6). This proportion was much smaller than the 61 per cent who, in response to a direct query, reported having "heard something" about how the election was going by the time they went to cast their ballots. Though the later a person voted, the more opportunity he evidently had to follow returns beforehand, we found no evidence of anyone having intentionally delayed going to the polls until he could first hear returns in order to then decide whether and how to vote. On the contrary, the whole pattern of relationships between exposure and time of voting suggests that time of voting determined the time a person began following returns, rather than the other way around.

How do those who followed returns before making their vote decision differ from those who did not? Answering this question in a meaningful way is somewhat tricky, because a factor like education, which is known to be related to communication exposure, may, if it is also related to time of voting, be the real explanation for any relationship between following returns and other characteristics that go together with education. Within this sample of voters, we found a slight tendency for persons with less education to vote in the late afternoon rather than in the early evening, a tendency that could result in our attributing an effect to education that should more accurately be attributed to the effect of voting time on exposure. Given this tendency, the near-identical proportions of college and non-college respondents who had followed returns (Table 2.7) implies that the effect of

---

[8] This statistic squares remarkably well with the 41 per cent of Californians voting after 4:30 P.M. found by Mendelsohn (*op. cit.*, p. 219) to have been exposed to election broadcasts before voting. It does not square with Fuch's finding (*op. cit.*, p. 234) of about 1 of 5, which can be calculated from information he gives in Table 6; the proportion there is of all persons who went to the polls after 1:00 P.M.

education on exposure may actually be negative. We can at least be confident that it is *not* the longer schooling that accounts for the pre-voting exposure of late voters.

It *is* our impression that the pre-voting exposure to network returns expressed primarily a spectator orientation, rather than an effort to obtain politically relevant information. This impression came from our examination of why people chose a particular channel or station. It received some additional but mild support from several comparisons summarized in Table 2.7. First, and understandably, persons who described themselves as having paid "a great deal of attention" to the campaign were distinctly more prone to have followed returns than those reporting "some" or "little and no interest." Yet any relationship between interest and exposure disappears altogether when importance attached to the outcome of the election is used as the criterion of interest. Late voters who thought that who won would make a "great deal of difference" *and* considered the 1964 election "more important than most presidential elections" were no more likely to have followed returns before voting than those with no great stake in the election. The avidity with which many persons follow the developments of a political campaign, regardless of whether or not they attach any great importance to the outcome, suggests that what keeps them close to their radio or television set on election day is not so much their desire for politically useful information as either their addiction to viewing (or listening) or their concern about missing some important development, some "good play" perhaps.

Pursuing these clues, we find that voters who had been expecting either a close presidential race, or an extremely close Senate contest within their state, had about the same pre-voting exposure to network broadcasts. In neither case is the difference reliable, but it once again contradicts the notion that most exposure represents a deliberate effort to seek information necessary to clarify a highly ambiguous situation.

There was a slight negative relationship between political confidence and pre-voting exposure to network election broadcasts. Political confidence in this study was measured by agreement with three separate items: "People like me don't have any say

Table 2.7 People who Followed Returns Before Voting

	*Number of Respondents**	*Percentage Who Followed Returns*
Education		
At least some college	195	39
Never attended college	164	42
	359	
Attention paid to campaign		
Great deal	150	49
Some	150	36
Little and none	62	31
	362	
Importance of election		
Very important	192	39
Not very important	147	40
	339	
Expectation of close presidential vote		
Both nationally and in state	32	31
Nationally or in state	115	41
In neither	195	42
	342	
Expectation of Senate vote		
Extremely close	151	42
All others	195	39
	346	
Political confidence		
High	167	36
Low	193	44
	360	
Candidate vs. party orientation		
Candidate orientation	278	38
Party orientation	79	49
	357	
Straight vs. split-ticket voters		
Split-ticket	62	31
Straight	266	42
	328	
Motivational conflict		
Anti-Goldwater Republicans	93	40
Goldwater Republicans	57	39
Others	212	41
	362	

*Does not include respondents on whom adequate information was not obtained.

Table 2.7 Continued

	*Number of Respondents**	*Percentage Who Followed Returns*
Politically deviant residents		
Deviants	74	41
Nondeviants	157	43
Swing precincts and independents	131	37
	362	
Presidential vote		
Johnson	209	39
Goldwater	123	42
	332	

*Does not include respondents on whom adequate information was not obtained.

about what the government does"; "Sometimes politics and government seem so complicated that a person like me can't really understand what's going on"; and "So many people vote in an election that it rarely matters whether one votes or not."[9] Agreement with any one of these items indicated low political confidence relative to the rest of the sample. Those low in political confidence were somewhat more likely to have followed network returns before voting, presumably waiting for the spectacle to unfold.

Party orientation is generally a factor that promotes stability and works against ticket splitting. Voters who said that in this election they found the choice between the candidates distinctly more important than the choice between the two parties were somewhat less likely to have been following returns before voting. The same was true of persons who voted for presidential and senatorial candidates of opposite parties. These ticket splitters followed returns less often than party regulars.

Anti-Goldwater Republicans, who represented a fairly large group of voters subject to motivational cross-pressures, had no more pre-voting exposure to network returns than consistent Goldwater supporters or registered Democrats. Similarly, party registrants residing in an area in which registrants for the other

[9] Angus Campbell *et al.*, *The American Voter* (New York: John Wiley & Sons, 1960), from where these items were adapted.

party clearly predominated (e.g., registered Republicans in solidly Democratic precincts) had about the same amount of pre-voting exposure as voters whose party registrations coincided with that of the majority in their district.

On the whole, then, the pre-voting audience to the election broadcasts seemed, if anything, to include more people consistent in their voting preference and stable in their political allegiances. There is no evidence that partisan political factors determined exposure.

Finally, we look at the vote for president. The proportion of Johnson and Goldwater voters who followed returns before voting is just about the same, lending no support to the proposition that, among these *late* voters, those for Johnson might have gleefully sought out the information that those for Goldwater sought deliberately to avoid.

All this minimizes the probability that exposure to returns was politically motivated or had political effects of any great magnitude; as we have said, the interest in returns appears to have contained an important component of spectatorship. Certainly they were *not* followed by people for the deliberate purpose of obtaining information on which to base their vote decision, and we failed to locate a single person among this California sample of late voters who had held off voting so that he could first hear some significant results.

To some extent, these observations bear on the law of minimal consequences. Persons who did follow returns before voting had, on the average, a somewhat greater interest in the political campaign and were, perhaps for that reason, more likely to have made up their minds. On the whole, the pre-voting audience included slightly, but not significantly, more people who were oriented toward a party symbol and less likely to split their tickets. These factors tend to promote stability. In addition, most politically alert persons are better able to forecast the outcome in advance than those with less interest. In the next chapter, therefore, we shall take a closer look at how late voters who had correctly anticipated the outcome of the election differed, in both their exposure and their reactions to early returns, from those whose expectations were invalidated.

3

Landslide Perceptions: The Effect of Exposure and Expectations

By late afternoon on election day in 1964, the landslide dimensions of the Johnson victory should have been plain to anyone who had heard election news and was ready to draw the obvious conclusion. Information pointing to a landslide was forthcoming from a number of sources, not just from network election broadcasts. The questions here concern how many late voters saw the election as already decided by the time they went to the polls, and what information, including that to which they were exposed before election day, was primarily responsible for this conclusion. Before one can even try to determine whether the amount of nonvoting in California, or the way the late vote there went, was affected in any way by the early onset of the election coverage by the networks, one must separate the impact of the various sources of news about the election.

Sources of Information

Each late voter was asked directly whether, by the time he voted (or, in the case of nonvoters, before poll closing time), he had

Table 3.1 Conclusions from Returns Heard Before Voting*

Conclusion Drawn	*California*		*Ohio*	
	N	%	N	%
Johnson "had won," certain to win	123	34	9	8
Johnson ahead, would probably win	36	10	4	3
No conclusion, returns not significant	55	15	3	3
Goldwater ahead, doing well	6	2	0	0
Respondents with pre-voting perceptions	220	61	16	14
No information about returns	135	37	99	85
No answer	9	2	1	1
Total	364	100	116	100

*For nonvoters, the reference is to returns heard before polls had closed.

"heard something about how the race for the presidency was going." As Table 3.1 shows, the majority of late voters in California had heard something, but what is even more impressive is that when each was asked to recall as nearly as possible what it was that he had actually heard and to specify "what these things . . . indicated about who would win the election," a third of the entire California sample — and over half of those with any information — reported that they had reached the definite conclusion that Johnson, if he had not already won, was sure to be the winner. The definitive character of election news heard before voting is further emphasized by the small number who, notwithstanding the returns coming in, remained steadfast in their belief that Goldwater seemed to be doing well or still stood a good chance of being elected. There were only six such persons among the 220 who had heard something about returns before going to the polls. One of these was a very old woman, a bedridden nonvoter, who went to sleep secure in her belief that Goldwater had won. The others, according to what they said, were reluctant to draw conclusions from less than complete returns.

These observations are conclusive in one respect: An unusually large number of voters went to the polls (or sat out the election) feeling certain that Johnson had won. Yet neither all the information nor all the certainty on the outcome characterizing California late voters came directly from network election broadcasts, which went on the air at 4:00 P.M. their time. To begin with, a small but nevertheless significant percentage of late voters interviewed in Ohio also said that they had heard or seen something that gave them an idea of how the election was going while they could still make a vote decision, and 8 per cent actually claimed to have been certain of the outcome by the time they voted. This 8 per cent may represent the number of persons who, after the fact and whatever the circumstances, would claim that they knew the outcome in advance. In any event, their conclusion, as they reported it, could not possibly have come from the network broadcasts, as these began only after polls in Ohio had closed.

These statistics from Ohio call attention to the impact of all types of election news available to the electorate before polls close. Late voters in both states, but particularly those in California (as we can surmise from Table 3.2), obtained much information from non-network broadcasts and regular news programs, from newspapers, and by word of mouth. It therefore stands to reason that, even without the early start of full network coverage, a greater proportion of late voters in California than in

Table 3.2 Conclusion from Returns by Source

Most Important Source of Returns	*Total Citing Each Source*		*"Certains" Citing Each Source*	
	N	%	N	%*
Television	88	40	55	63
Radio	91	41	51	56
Persons	34	15	15	44
Newspapers	7	3	2	29
All sources	220	99†	123	56
Before voting:				
Followed network returns	146	40	79	54
Did not follow network returns	218	60	44	20
	364	100	123	34

*The percentages in this column are those of all persons citing a particular source who became "certain."

†Due to rounding.

Ohio would have had some idea of how the race was shaping up by the time they went to the polls. The later hour at which Californians were voting gave them a chance to hear election news from more parts of the country; the election trends available by the time polls closed would naturally offer a more complete picture. Without considering these other sources of news, one obviously cannot talk accurately about the influence specifically attributable to the early start of the continuous election coverage by the networks.

Radio and television were cited by 81 per cent of the Californians as the primary source of pre-voting information about the outcome. Actually the importance of the broadcast media — both the continuous coverage by the networks and earlier news bulletins — was undoubtedly even greater than indicated by this figure. An undetermined number of the 16 per cent who said "other persons" were their primary source of pre-voting election news must have been indirect recipients of news heard on radio or television.

Television, which lagged slightly behind radio in the number of mentions, appears to have been the news source most apt to make a person exposed to it certain of the election outcome. Radio was second, and "other persons" ran ahead of newspapers. That so many of those getting information from other persons should have become sure of the outcome suggests that many who themselves had become certain from the broadcast media passed on to others not only information they had received but also their convictions.

The important contribution of the network election coverage is nevertheless indicated by the large number who had been following these broadcasts for some time before they went to the polls and had become certain as a result. Not only is the proportion of "certains" among this group nearly three times as high as among those who had *not* been following the returns, but direct exposure to the broadcasts prior to voting accounts for almost two thirds of all of those assured that Johnson would win regardless of whether or how they themselves voted. Yet the forty-four persons who became certain without following the returns again point to the existence of indirect effects as well as to the influence of other news sources.

How much did the *time* a voter went to the polls affect what he already knew about the outcome? The later he went to the polls, the more opportunity he naturally had to follow returns before voting, and the more likely he was to have heard definitive returns from the presidential race as well as some early returns from the California Senate race (Table 3.3). More persons voting in the early evening had been following returns before voting than those voting late in the afternoon. Similarly, the proportion of "certains" among early-evening voters was higher than among those who went to the polls in the earlier periods.

To pin down the impact of the early election coverage, we asked every late voter who had followed the continuous election coverage *at any time* on election day, before or after he had cast his ballot, about his first impression upon tuning in: "Did you see or hear anything right away that gave you the idea that the race for president was more or less decided, or did you think for a while that the outcome was in doubt?" Eighty per cent said that they knew right away.

The precise amount of information available to a person on tuning into the network returns seems to have influenced his initial reaction very little. Among Californians who reported that they had begun following returns at 4:00 P.M. — the beginning of the continuous election coverage — 71 per cent said that they had immediately reached the conclusion Johnson had won. There is a striking parallel between this percentage and the 70 per cent in Ohio (where most viewers and listeners had their sets tuned to the network coverage from its start at 7:00 P.M. EST — equivalent to 4:00 P.M. California time) who likewise reported that they recognized right away, as soon as the first returns began coming in, that the election was more or less over.[1] The more

---

[1] We cannot, however, overlook the discrepancy observed in California responses to two entirely unrelated questions. On the one hand, we have this rather high proportion reporting their first impression from network returns, heard at 4:00 P.M. or shortly thereafter, was of a race pretty much decided; on the other hand, the much smaller percentage (54 per cent) of those following returns before voting who said they were certain of the out-

Table 3.3 Effect of Time of Voting on Exposure to Returns

	Voting Time								*Total Responses*	
	After 4:00 P.M. but by 5:30 P.M.		After 5:30 P.M. but by 6:30 P.M.		After 6:30 P.M.		Nonvoters			
	N	%	N	%	N	%	N	%	N	%
Heard some news before voting	64	44*	82	66	66	83	7	58	220	60
Certain of outcome	30	21	45	36	41	51	5	42	123	34
Followed network returns before voting	40	28	50	40	47	59	7	58	144	40
Exposed to California Senate returns	6	4	13	10	16	20	0	0	35	10
Total respondents voting within period	144		125		80		12		364	

*The proportions are those of all voters voting within the period, i.e., 64/144 = 44%. Columns cannot be added, because both multiple responses and non-responses are possible. For three persons exact time of voting was not established and accounts for the loss of cases when calculating the row sums.

important point is that the proportion rose only slightly among those who joined the audience at a later hour, after more complete returns had been tallied and after the networks had made their explicit predictions. For example, the same claim, that they knew right away, was advanced by 85 per cent of those in California who started to follow returns *after* 7:30 P.M., when it was probably too late to cast a vote if they had not already done so.

Respondents were also asked to specify precisely what they had heard before voting that led them to some conclusion about who would win. The many accounts of these pre-voting perceptions were classed into four categories, irrespective of the source from which these perceptions were obtained. The four categories are:

(1) *early returns*, often from only a few districts, or inferences from reports of turnout in certain bellweather areas;

(2) *returns from specific states,* such as one of the very large states with many electoral votes or one of the states that Goldwater needed to win if he were to win nationally;

(3) *predictions,* in the form of explicit declarations from computerized projections or based on what a commentator said; and

(4) *general trends in the returns,* either of the total vote or of the electoral vote.

Many respondents mentioned items in more than one category. A person might, for example, refer both to Johnson's having

---

come (by the time they went to vote). These represent responses to two questions coming in different portions of the interview, and document the difficulty of eliciting valid information on matters of this sort from a *post-factum* interview. No matter how careful one is in collecting data, the information one obtains rarely attains the degree of quantitative precision to measure a very small effect. The criterion by which we inferred "certainty before voting" from an open-ended response must have been more restrictive than seeing the race as more or less decided — as against its being pretty much in doubt — upon tuning in on the coverage. In our search for relationships between "certainty" and other factors, we have relied most heavily on the more restrictive indicator, but have not confined ourselves to it completely.

Table 3.4 Information Heard by Time of Voting

Voting Time	*Information Heard*								*Total Respondents Voting Within Period*
	Early Returns		*Specific States*		*Computer Predictions*		*General Trends*		
	N	%	N	%	N	%	N	%	N
After 4:00 P.M. but by 5:30 P.M.	26	18*	11	8	20	14	31	22	144
After 5:30 P.M. but by 6:30 P.M.	26	21	6	5	32	26	44	35	125
After 6:30 P.M.	14	18	13	16	24	38	48	60	80
Nonvoters†	2	16	0	0	0	0	7	58	12
Total respondents citing indicator	68	19	30	8	76	21	130	36	361††

*Inasmuch as a respondent might report more than one of these and a good many respondents had heard nothing, the row sums equal neither the total voting at the given time nor those voting at the time who were exposed. The percentage columns represent proportions among those voting at a given time who heard the specific information.

†For nonvoters, the reference is to all perceptions before polls closed.

††Does not include three persons from whom exact time of voting was not ascertained.

won New York and to a computerized projection as the clues on which he based his conclusion. Also, many respondents did not differentiate clearly between a prediction (or projection) and the actual tally by the networks of both the electoral and the popular vote. As a result, the influence of computerized projections is probably somewhat understated, and that of general trends in the count somewhat inflated.

That the time a respondent voted influenced the type of information he heard before voting is clearly shown in Table 3.4. Similar proportions of those voting in different periods mentioned hearing early returns, mostly from sources other than the network election broadcasts. Those voting later in the day had more opportunity to follow the election coverage by the networks and to hear definitive returns. Hence the overwhelming majorities for Johnson from practically all parts of the country (general trends) received increasingly frequent mention and emerged as the single most important indicator of the outcome, especially during the last hour and a half of voting. In every time period, the number of voters who mentioned computer-based predictions is much smaller than the number mentioning the actual returns.[2] Coincidentally, none of the twelve nonvoters referred to a computer prediction when recounting what he had heard before polls closed.

Nevertheless, the computer seems to be especially convincing among those whose attention it catches (Table 3.5). A higher proportion of those who mentioned computer predictions had become certain of the outcome before they went to the polls. However, interpret this datum with some caution, because time of voting, as we have seen, was related both to what a person was likely to have heard and to the likelihood of his having become certain. What appears as an influence of the computer may there-

---

[2] The 21 per cent who had heard computer predictions *before* voting should be compared with the highly misleading figure of 67 per cent obtained by Fuchs from a sample of 344 voters. His tabulation is based on 164 cases, less than half the sample. There is no explanation, but one infers that all who had not been radio or television listeners previous to voting were conveniently excluded. See Douglas A. Fuchs, "Election Day Newscasts and Their Effects on Western Voter Turnout," *Journalism Quarterly,* XLII (Winter 1965), p. 27.

Table 3.5 Information Heard and Perception of Outcome as Certain Before Voting

Information Heard	*Total Who Had Heard*		*Perceived Outcome as Certain Before Voting*	
	N	%	N	%*
Early returns	68	19	17	25
Specific states	30	8	22	73
Computer predictions	76	21	59	76
General trends	130	36	78	60
Total respondents	364			
Total "certain"			123	34

*The proportions are of those who heard given item of information who became "certain."

fore be a function of time of voting. Unfortunately our sample is too small to permit any hard-and-fast conclusions by examining the relationship between certainty and the information heard by persons casting ballots in each of the different time periods. Nevertheless, the persuasiveness of computers is underscored by a number of other observations.

At first glance, seeing the electoral votes of one or two critical states go into the Johnson column appears to have been nearly as effective as an explicit computer prediction; the comparable statistics are 73 and 76 per cent. Yet "specific states" were mentioned by relatively few respondents, and those who referred to these were most often the late-late voters, whose ballots were cast in the period after 6:30 P.M. Returns in by that time must have been conclusive and a person did not have to rely on a computer to become certain. The independent impact the computer had apart from the growing lead Johnson was amassing in the votes tallied is therefore difficult to gauge. Thus, some persons may have begun to sense the prospect of a Johnson victory from the general returns, but they became certain only after they heard an explicit prediction, or after some state they had expected to go Republican — Ohio for example — was shown to have given its sizeable electoral vote to Johnson. The strongest evidence for the effectiveness of the computer evidently lies in the number of mentions it received among the earlier voters. In the last time period, the number who mentioned the computer declined while the number who mentioned general trends rose both absolutely and proportionately. We infer that those who had become certain early more often did so because of an explicit prediction, while those during the later hours had much other information on which they could rely.

Reliance on Computers

The importance of computer-based predictions and of the declarations of a winner before most votes had been counted was undoubtedly minimized by the clear indications implicit in even the first significant returns. An issue that still remains to be resolved is the extent to which a voter's willingness to draw a definitive conclusion from incomplete returns heard before voting hinges on the cues to which he is primarily oriented. As far as 1964 is concerned, this issue boils down essentially to the importance of computer-based projections *vis-à-vis* the confirmation that early returns gave to advance expectations that Goldwater had little chance of winning. The 1964 data do not permit any conclusions about the persuasiveness of computers, had the returns been ambiguous in their implication or had the prediction clearly contradicted advance expectations. Still, we can examine the reactions of those who found the computer "most helpful" and, subsequently, the role of expectations, involvement, and preferences.

Besides asking those with pre-voting perceptions what they had actually heard before they went to the polls, we also asked every respondent who had followed network election broadcasts *at any time,* before or after voting, which of seven items in the broadcasts they had found "most helpful in giving [them] an idea of how the election was going." Respondents were also encouraged to mention anything not included among the original seven choices. When the responses of all who followed returns were tabulated, the "actual count of the popular vote" and the "tally of electoral votes" by the networks shared top honors, each receiving about one third of all choices. "Computer predictions" came next with about one sixth, while "interpretations by commentators and reporters" ran a poor fourth with about 5 per cent of all mentions. Other items received hardly any mentions at all. The weak showing of commentary in this context may come as a surprise, since respondents seemed to have attached such great importance to commentators when it came to choosing a network or channel for viewing (see Table 2.5). It implies, as already suggested, that the commentator's style and personality are deemed more important than the expertise with which he appears to analyze returns. The latter seems to be perceived not so much in personal terms as in terms of an impersonal organization and of technology.

The power of the computer to compel a definite conclusion is underlined again when we consider the responses of only those with pre-voting perceptions. Persons who considered the computer "most helpful" had become certain more often than persons who found some other element in the telecast of greater help (Table 3.6). Though based on a relatively small number of cases, this observation reinforces the prior conclusion based on the kind of information a person had heard before voting.

Though the computer was an important cue for a small number of people, the popular vote count and the tally of electoral votes seem to have convinced *more* people and thus had a greater

Table 3.6 Effect of Item "Most Helpful" on Conclusion from Returns

Conclusion Drawn	*Item "Most Helpful"*							
	Popular Vote Count		*Electoral Vote Tally*		*Computerized Predictions*		*All Other Items*	
	N	%	N	%	N	%	N	%
Johnson, certain	37	51	42	57	26	70	6	33
Johnson, probably	11	15	10	14	5	14	5	28
No conclusion, Goldwater ahead, etc.	24	33	21	29	6	16	6	39
Total respondents citing item	72	99†	73	100	37	100	18	100

*Includes only respondents (1) who had pre-voting perceptions of how the race for president was going, (2) who had followed network returns at some time on election day, and (3) on whom full information on the items "most helpful" was obtained.
†Due to rounding.

impact, probably because vote tabulations gave a clear indication of the winner and were continuously before people's eyes. Computers soon took a back seat. Thus, those who had found computer predictions most helpful constitute only 23 per cent of all those certain, while the popular vote count and the tally of electoral votes *together* accounted for a full 71 per cent.

Unfortunately we cannot be at all sure of the ability of every respondent to distinguish clearly between a computer-based projection and the use of other devices for a rapid tally of votes. Some were probably not aware that the tally of the electoral vote reflected projections from highly incomplete totals of the vote in many states. Accordingly, we must note that those who did rely on computers had as a rule more accurate knowledge of the capabilities of computers; for that reason, these persons may also have been better able to understand how the outcome of a race could be correctly forecast even with most of the popular vote still uncounted. As a matter of fact, a few respondents were both puzzled and hostile to computers. Still harking back to the California primary, they expressed bewilderment and dismay that the election could possibly have been declared for Goldwater while Rockefeller was clearly ahead in the actual count.

If reliance on computer predictions is indeed a function of what a person understands about the use of the computer in making forecasts, we may again be dealing with a spurious relationship. The same sophistication that is revealed in a person's knowledge of the computer and that leads him to find it "most helpful" could also account for his ability to draw on his own, from incomplete returns, the "obvious" conclusion that Johnson was sure to win. Whether or not reliance on the computer has an independent effect on this conclusion is difficult to check out. However, when college attendance is used as an indicator of sophistication, those who had attended were *no more* likely to cite the computer than those who had not; on the other hand, more college people had had some information before voting on how the race was shaping up, and if they had heard something, they were also more likely to become certain of the outcome as a consequence. It does appear, therefore, that computerized projections had some impact over and above what persons discerned from the returns. Even in this election, where all signs pointed in the same direction, computers may have exerted an important supplementary influence by lending assurance that the conclusion drawn from the vote count was indeed correct.

Acceptance of computer-based predictions also encounters resistance from certain attitudes indicating an unwillingness to let the computers have their due. Persons who cited the computer as "most helpful" were *less* apt than others to think that early computer-based predictions "took the fun out of election night." They were also more emphatic in their *rejection* of the statement that computers were more often wrong than right. In part, the skepticism toward the computer expressed in this statement could have been the result of displaced disappointment, particularly among Goldwater supporters who wanted to maintain their hope for victory and therefore went out of their way to inoculate themselves against the potentially persuasive influence of these new gadgets.

Involvement, Preferences, and Expectations

It is difficult to generalize from the 1964 election about the potential effects of computers; as indicated, the popular vote count, the electoral vote tally, and the computer-based predictions confirmed one another. The conclusion that Johnson would win was inescapable to anyone willing to read the portents. Many persons had in fact reached this conclusion before the election, so that the returns and the predictions merely confirmed what they expected. Under circumstances when pre-election forecasts and early returns do not delineate a consistently unambiguous picture of the probable outcome, the impact of explicitly computer-based projections and of early returns could be rather different. A person's preferences and expectations, as affected by his involvement in the election, would be related to his readiness to draw a conclusion and to his acceptance of computer-based predictions, particularly where the election was expected to be close and the returns indicated a "cliff-hanger".

Common sense suggests that the impact of early returns on perceptions of the outcome would be greatest among people convinced of the importance of the election. Their concern would provide them with a strong motive for attending to the returns in order to discern any indications of the eventual outcome. This line of reasoning is not supported by data already presented in Chapter 2. They show rather that persons who had paid a "great deal" of attention to the pre-election campaign followed returns before voting more often than those who had paid less attention, but that the degree of involvement in the outcome of the election made no difference in this regard. Table 3.7 reveals the effect of involvement on pre-voting perceptions of election trends to be equally small. Having heard some election news or having become "certain" before voting was only slightly more frequent among persons who considered the outcome unusually important than among those who attributed no special significance to who won.

Even a moment's reflection will bring to mind the reasons. Any direct relationship between involvement and recognizing that the election was all but over is vitiated by the interplay of expectations, preferences, and the willingness to accept the indicated outcome. Studies of prior elections have certainly suggested that vote intentions are related to pre-election expectations.[3]

Table 3.7 Effect of Importance of the Election on Conclusion from Returns

Conclusion Drawn	*Election Important*		*Election Not So Important*	
	N	%	N	%
Johnson, certain	71	59	48	55
Johnson, probable	20	17	14	16
No conclusion, Goldwater ahead, etc.	30	25	25	29
Total with some news before voting	121	100	87	100
All late voters and nonvoters*	193		147	
% of total "certain"		37		31
% of total with some news		63		59

*Includes only respondents on whom complete information was obtained.

[3] Bernard Berelson *et al.*, *Voting* (Chicago: The University of Chicago Press, 1954), p. 289.

Even in the aftermath of this clearly one-sided election, many Goldwater voters were ready to admit that they had greatly overestimated their candidate's chance of winning and of carrying their own state. One out of five Goldwater voters said that before the election he had believed his man was the front-runner, or at least had an equal chance of beating Johnson; but only one out of fifteen for Johnson conceded that he had feared the race might be extremely close, and almost none said that he had believed Johnson was running behind. Looked at from the opposite side, two thirds (68 per cent) of the Johnson voters had been expecting their man to win in a race that was "not at all close," but only somewhat over one third (38 per cent) of the Republican faithfuls had come to terms with the prospect that they were about to lose by a rather large margin.

Despite the partially projective nature of these expectations, the element of realism was not lacking. Very few Republicans or Democrats went on record as having believed that Goldwater's chances were better than Johnson's.[4] These expectations were in

---

[4] There is good justification for raising questions about the validity of data on pre-election expectations as reported after the fact. Faulty recollections by voters and rationalizations to the effect that they knew all along that the man who did win was a sure winner, will inevitably cause some distortion in their responses, (see Herbert H. Hyman, *Survey Design and Analysis*), the exact magnitude of which is difficult to estimate. Nevertheless, we have reason to believe that the responses of late voters have at least some relationship to what they did expect. The relation between expectations and preferences showed up in both states. It was even stronger in Ohio, where more late voters said that they had expected Johnson to win and to carry their own state, and where fewer said that they had believed the electoral votes of their own state might be crucial to the outcome. The greater assuredness in Ohio about Johnson's chances reflects the heavy representation of Johnson supporters among the late voters in that state.

When we compare expectations regarding the outcome of the Senate race in the two states, the effect of preference on reports of what respondents had anticipated turns out to be stronger than that of who actually won. A close Senate race had been predicted in both states, and a majority of the late voters in each admitted afterwards that they had been wrong in their pre-election estimates. In California, where the Republican won, 56 per cent said that they had expected the Democrat to win, whereas in Ohio, where the Democrat won, a near-identical 58 per cent acknowledged that they had been wrong in anticipating a Republican victory. Such admission by majorities in both states reassures us that most of them were not just

good part shaped by reports in the news media. Persons who had attended college or who were heavy consumers of news were found to be more accurate in their pre-election expectations than others. By contrast, the political atmosphere within the neighborhood where the voter resided had no residual effect on expectations. For example, Goldwater voters residing in solidly Democratic precincts were no more likely to have forecast a Johnson victory than Goldwater voters in precincts that were Republican strongholds.

This inference — that expectations were shaped by media reports of polls and predictions, and modified by political preferences — is generally confirmed by other studies. However, the finding that the immediate environment had no discernible effect on expectations contradicts an explicit conclusion from a 1940 study that face-to-face contacts were slightly more important than the formal mass media.[5] While we recognize that our data on expectations, collected as they were *after* the election, are not the most reliable indicators of what people's assessments *had* been, it is a fact that since 1940 pre-election polls have become more reliable and their findings more widely publicized. Hence it stands to reason that the impact of published polls is greater today than it was at that time.

Whatever the effect of preferences and the information environment on expectations formed before election day 1964, the impact of the news coverage on pre-voting perceptions of the outcome was certainly compelling. The rather minor difference in the conclusions drawn by the supporters of the two candidates (Table 3.8) is all the more noteworthy since the news meant something rather different to each group. Apparently the early information was sufficiently conclusive to almost wipe out the influence of political preferences. An identical proportion in both groups had become certain of the outcome, but where information received did not lead to certainty, Goldwater supporters

---

second-guessing and that responses to queries about prior expectations, undertaken after the election, possess at least some validity.

[5] Paul F. Lazarsfeld *et al.*, *The People's Choice* (New York: Columbia University Press, 1948).

Table 3.8 Conclusion from Returns by Vote for President

Conclusion Drawn	*Goldwater*		*Johnson*		*Abstained*		*Refused Answer*	
	N	%	N	%	N	%	N	%
Johnson, certain	43	54	69	55	8	89	3	43
Johnson, probably	10	13	26	21	0	—	0	—
No conclusion, Goldwater ahead, etc.	26	33	30	24	1	11	4	57
Total with some news before voting	79	100	125	100	9	100	7	100
All late voters and nonvoters	123		211		15		15	
% of total "certain"		35		33		53		20
% of total with some news		64		59		60		47

were somewhat more inclined than Johnson supporters to draw no conclusion at all. What wishful thinking there was among Goldwater supporters took the form of an express desire not to give up hope, though this was in all probability more or less balanced by caution among Johnson voters, a fear of premature rejoicing in the form of a "don't count your chickens" reaction.

Expectations would also have an impact on conclusions drawn, particularly because they were linked with preferences. Thus an accurate expectation would have rather different significance for the supporters of each candidate. Democrats would hardly be in need of reassurance, while Goldwater Republicans might be strongly motivated to avoid as long as possible any news that could only be unpleasant. However, as far as those exposed to some election news were concerned, we needed to test the influence of expectations on the readiness with which persons drew conclusions from early and partial returns.

Thus, we reasoned specifically that the amount of information needed to confirm an expectation would be less than that required to invalidate it. We furthermore reasoned that the impact of early returns on pre-voting perceptions would be least on those anticipating a Johnson landslide, there being no element of surprise. At the same time, as we have noted, expectations are linked to preferences which these expectations tend to support. This linkage could provide a motivational basis for resisting invalidating evidence—e.g., Goldwater supporters bolstered by the expectation of a Republican victory would overlook the omens of impending defeat. Similarly, the existence of a relationship between preferences and a conclusion that Johnson was certain to win would suggest that Goldwaterites were able to maintain a bandwagon psychology by discounting the evidence of the returns, just as many of them had been inclined to distrust and therefore explain away the advance predictions of pollsters and political analysts.

The effect of expectations on "certainty" (Table 3.9) is stronger than that of political preferences. The proportion of those exposed who became certain was highest among those who expected a Johnson walkaway victory. This effect is not due to differential exposure, as the proportions in the top row refer

Table 3.9 Effect of Pre-election Day Expectations on Conclusion from Returns

	Pre-Election Expectations					
Conclusion Drawn	*Goldwater or Extremely Close*		*Johnson Fairly Close*		*Johnson Not Close at All*	
	N	%	N	%	N	%
Johnson, certain	10	45	29	48	79	63
Johnson, probably	4	18	12	20	19	15
No conclusion, Goldwater ahead, etc.	8	36	20	33	27	22
Total with some news before voting	22	99†	61	101†	125	100
All late voters and nonvoters*	45		101		187	
% of total "certain"		22		29		42
% of total with some news		49		60		71

*Includes only persons on whom complete information was obtained.
†Due to rounding.

only to those who had "heard something." Still, pre-voting exposure to returns was greater among those who had correctly assessed the outcome in advance than among the other two groups, i.e., those who thought Johnson would win in a close race and those who had given Goldwater a near-even chance or better. Nothing in these data indicates that persons most in doubt about the probable outcome felt impelled to seek out information either in order to resolve the ambiguity or to make up their minds on how to vote.

Again one might argue that much of this was second–guessing, that some persons saying they knew the outcome by the time they went to vote would also be inclined to claim they had known what it would be all along. However, in line with reasoning advanced before, we would hold that the effect of expectations on the conclusion drawn is greatest where the information is most ambiguous, and that the availability of clear information tends to weaken the effect of expectations. The experimental literature certainly shows how much the perception of ambiguous stimuli depends on the psychological set of the subject interpreting the object or situation. With regard to election returns, conclusions drawn from scanty information would vary in relation to who was *expected* to win. These same expectations would have less influence on responses to full information about returns from all over the country.

This hypothesis can be tested against two sets of data: the first impressions obtained by persons who began following the network election broadcasts at different times, and the conclusions drawn by persons who did and who did not follow these broadcasts before voting.

In both California and Ohio, we found a highly reliable difference between the first impressions of persons who had pretty much counted on Johnson's winning and of those who had given Goldwater a chance in either an extremely close or a wide-open race. The difference shows up despite the possible effect of the time at which these first impressions were obtained. We next divided all California viewers into those who had begun following returns before 5:00 P.M. and those who had not begun until 5:00 P.M. or later. All three networks had declared Johnson the winner before this time, and the returns coming in thereafter were so definitely one-sided that it would have been difficult for anyone paying careful attention not to become immediately convinced. Accordingly, we can treat the pre-5:00 P.M. group as exposed to relatively ambiguous information; the post-5:00 P.M., as exposed to clearly convincing evidence.

A comparison of the coefficients of association (Kendall's Q) between "starting to follow returns by 5:00 P.M." and "reaching an immediate conclusion that the race was pretty much decided" shows that the degree of ambiguity made a greater difference among those who had given Goldwater a chance to win than among the others. The value of the coefficient for the first group was —.43; it was —.24 for those who had never thought the race would even be close. Among persons joining the audience from 5:00 P.M. on, expectations mattered much less than they had before.

The same comparison was made between persons who had been following network election returns for at least a half hour before casting a vote and those whose pre-voting perceptions came from a source other than the network broadcasts. It is our assumption that network broadcasts provided news that was comparatively less ambiguous, and that therefore the effect of expectations would be greater among persons whose information came from other sources. The coefficient of association between certainty and expectations returns was .44 for persons whose information was obtained from a variety of sources, such as news bulletins, conversations, and so forth; it was .20 for those who had been following the election coverage of the networks.

The impact of *inconclusive* returns is thus limited insofar as the conclusions people draw will be influenced by what they have been expecting to happen. The more definitive the information in the returns, the greater its capacity to upset expectations.

Implications for Specific Types of Elections

As we have tried to show, the impact of early returns on pre-voting perceptions of the outcome depends in large measure on information available, including information (especially what polls predict) to which late voters have been exposed even before an election takes place. In the 1964 election, there were few individuals who had given Goldwater at least an even chance and then had found out, before they went to vote, that he was about to suffer an overwhelming defeat. Because the pre-election predictions were so unanimous, only a small number could possibly experience an invalidation before they went to the polls. But this would not be the case in every election.

In other elections, in 1960 for instance, the pollsters did not venture beyond the prediction of an extremely close race. If predictions are one-sided and the same front-runner is clearly indicated by all, the early returns can supply information that either confirms or contradicts the expectations derived from predictions, or is so ambiguous that everyone is free to draw his own conclusion. If, on the other hand, pre-election predictions point to a close race, early returns may or may not clarify the ambiguity.

In the following diagram, several types of elections are presented schematically. The key words in each box describe the predominant impact of the early returns under the conditions of the specific type of election.

		Pre-Election Predictions:	
		One-Sided Race	Close Race
Early Returns:	Clear	I. Confirm III. Contradict	II. Clarify
	Ambiguous	IV. Unresolved	V. Confirm—unresolved

Types I and V occur in elections in which early returns essentially confirm predictions, and invalidating perceptions will therefore be rare. At the same time, Type V is very much like Type IV in that the implications of early returns are ambiguous. Under these conditions we would expect the conclusions drawn from returns to be very strongly influenced by expectations. Their direct impact would be minimized as a consequence. The potential for broadcast influence appears to be greatest in election Types II and III, where early returns either indicate a winner of a race expected to be close or indicate that the expected winner will lose. These two types of election situations ought to be the subject of special concern. The improvement of polling techniques since the fiasco of 1948 is apt to preclude the reoccurrence of Type III elections. However, the extreme caution exhibited by pollsters in the aftermath of 1948 suggests that the Type II situation will increase in frequency — especially as the use of computers for projections also becomes more sophisticated, more reliable, and speedier. At any rate, the impact of early returns on pre-voting perceptions is closely linked to the accuracy of forecasts by pollsters.

Nevertheless, there will always be voters whose own expectations differ from those disseminated by the mass media. Mavericks, whose expectations are invalidated, will be found in every election. To the extent that these persons respond to invalidating information by changing their prior intent to vote for a particular candidate, or to vote at all, they are always a source of potential instability. On the other hand, to the extent that these persons are less informed because less involved and therefore less likely to pay attention to or draw conclusions from early returns, the potential for behavioral changes is limited. The next two chapters look at the changes in electoral behavior observed in this study of broadcast effects.

4

Nonvoting and the Nonvoter

Propositions on voter turnout are of two broad types: One emphasizes the structural determinants of voting and nonvoting; the other, the social-psychological ones. When viewed in structural terms, different levels of electoral participation appear to be fairly stable attributes of the political system, reflecting the influence of cultural, historical, and social factors that operate independently of the candidates, specific issues, and other circumstances surrounding a particular election. The social-psychological approach tends to highlight the more specific motivational factors, whose strength varies from election to election, to explain differences and changes in voter-turnout rates. It inquires into the possible effects of specific perceptions and concrete events. How close the election is expected to be or how much importance people attach to the outcome presumably has some effect on the decisions of individuals to vote or not vote. Insofar as there is a dichotomy between structural and social-psychological approaches to voting behavior, this study of broadcast-induced effects represents an inquiry into the social psychology of voting.

A sharp line of division between the two approaches is nevertheless hard to maintain whenever one makes a serious attempt to understand what happened in a particular election. Structural and social-psychological influences have a way of confounding one another. Unless this is thoroughly understood, there will be a strong temptation not to take into full account the characteristics of the electoral system, and to attribute to specific and variable influences what may in reality be a structural effect. In this chapter we shall be greatly concerned about disentangling the two as we try to answer the question: How much nonvoting in California was a direct response to the dissemination of returns, via the network election coverage, indicating to people before they cast ballots that Johnson was winning by a landslide? In other words, did the returns have a slackening effect on the late vote?

Late-Election-Day Slack

The hypothesis of slack as a broadcast effect derives from a theory of politics: In a close electoral contest, where both parties believe they have an equal chance of winning, electioneering efforts will be intensified inasmuch as a relatively small number of votes may mark the difference between victory and defeat.[1] Every single vote counts. Accordingly, information received prior to voting that the race was no longer close, or that Johnson "had won," would make any additional vote less significant; Johnson votes were no longer necessary to assure his victory, and Goldwater supporters could do nothing to stave off the disaster. Consequently, the reasoning goes, individual voters upon hearing such news would be inclined to decide that going to the polls was futile, while party workers would likewise slacken in their efforts to get out the vote.

"As a general rule in American politics," Gosnell wrote in 1927, "the proportion of eligible voters that come to the polls varies directly with the closeness of the election in the particu-

---

[1] On this point, see Lewis A. Dexter, "The Use of Public Opinion Polls by Political Party Organizations," *Public Opinion Quarterly*, XVIII (Spring 1954), pp. 53–61. Raymond E. Wolfinger, "The Influence of Precinct Work on Voting Behavior," *Public Opinion Quarterly*, XXVII (Fall 1963), pp. 387–98, shows the efforts by party workers to be more important in local than in national elections, since patronage is at stake. On the general theory, see especially Anthony Downs, *An Economic Theory of Politics* (New York: Harper & Row, 1957).

lar jurisdiction analyzed. The general impression — that the election is going to be a close one — is sufficient to stimulate greatly the interest of electors in the voting process."[2] He supported the proposition by pointing to the close association that existed between the per cent of votes cast for the majority party in a state and the per cent of its eligible voters not voting in the 1920 and 1924 national elections. His tabulations appear to show that the greater the dominance by one party, the smaller the number who turn out. Yet in drawing his conclusions, Gosnell does not discuss the possibility that in some states and localities the dominance of one party might be maintained by an electoral system that systematically discourages many voters from registering and puts other obstacles in the way of voting. In the Southern United States and in some urban areas, low turnout is probably as much a cause as a consequence of one-party dominance. A more recent study in Indiana, using units smaller than a state, showed that a rise in voter participation within a particular district, as well as differences between districts, are less strongly affected by the competitiveness of the electoral situation than by the prestige of the office and the number of offices being contested in the election.[3]

Whatever the effect of the competitive factor, political folklore has it that close races make for high turnout and races that are not close make for slack. Voter turnout in 1964 fell somewhat below 63.1 per cent, the official estimate for the Kennedy-Nixon election of 1960. The decline from that high can probably be attributed to a slack that must have set in long before election day. The pre-election polls had indicated a clear victory for Johnson, and the majority of voters seemed to have accepted this prognosis. The fact that neither candidate in 1964 could match Kennedy or Nixon in appeal may also have had something to do with the lower turnout. Nevertheless, the certainty of many late voters in California before they went to the polls

---

[2] Harold F. Gosnell, *Getting Out the Vote: an Experiment in the Stimulation of Voting* (Chicago: The University of Chicago Press, 1927), p. 3.

[3] J. A. Robinson and W. H. Standing, "Some Correlates of Voter Participation in Indiana," *Journal of Politics*, XXII (February 1960), pp. 96–111.

that the election was already decided could be expected to reinforce and strengthen any prior disinclination to vote and even discourage some others who had expected the race to be close. But any slack directly attributable to the early broadcast of returns would have to be over and above the slack that had already occurred during the campaign, as all signs pointed to a rather lopsided Johnson victory. *To test for the existence of late-election-day slack, we looked for evidence that voters who had planned to vote, and would have voted, were dissuaded from casting ballots by what they heard about the returns.*

As a first step in this direction, we compared the rates of voter turnout in our roughly comparable samples of California and Ohio precincts in order to see whether there was an appreciable difference, one that could perhaps be attributed to the network broadcasts available to late voters in California but not in Ohio. We obtained official records of the number of registered persons who did and did not vote in each of the precincts. From these records it appears that *the nonvoting rate among registered voters in the California precincts (14 per cent) was slightly lower, not higher, than in the Ohio precincts (16 per cent).* The hypothesis of late-election-day slack in response to early election news fails to receive substantiation from these particular data.

Before commenting further on these nonvoting rates, we must summarize some findings of past studies relevant to our interpretation, bearing on the legal and institutional obstacles to a 100 per cent turnout. Our experiences in locating nonvoters convince us that the impact of election day broadcasts on electoral participation can be correctly assayed only within such a context.

Political Participation and Its Measures

Specific voting requirements are most concretely related to political participation. Particularly in the United States, where residence, literacy, and other requirements for full *de facto* qualification as an eligible voter vary considerably from state to state, and even between political subdivisions within the same state, it is rather difficult, if not impossible, to ascertain the precise number who are legally eligible in the sense that they *could* qualify as voters if only they chose to register. Thus, "raw turnout" is generally measured as the proportion of *citizens of voting age* who cast ballots — as in the two studies of "competitiveness" cited.

Take as an example the election of 1956, a typical "slack election." No serious political analyst raised the least doubt that President Eisenhower's re-election was anything but a foregone conclusion. No one seemed puzzled by the drop in electoral participation from its previous high to about 60 per cent of citizens of voting age. In seeking to explain why 38 million of the close to 100 million eligibles did not vote, Clinton Rossiter[4] cites figures indicating that:

(1) six million in the South were effectively kept from voting by a host of discriminatory practices, including literacy tests and the poll tax;

(2) five million failed to meet residence and other legal requirements for full qualification as voters;

(3) 600,000 residents of the District of Columbia had for years been deprived of the franchise;

(4) 600,000 were inmates of institutions and so could not vote; and

(5) some 300,000 were serving in the armed forces and were without a voting residence in the United States.

These 12.5 million "eligible" notvoters account for about a third of those not voting, and must immediately be eliminated from all calculations if we wish to obtain any basis for a reliable estimate about the number who deliberately sat out the election or were too apathetic to vote. The raw turnout figure invariably exaggerates the influence of social-psychological factors and the possibility of increasing turnout by whipping up voter interest.

This problem of what voter-turnout figures mean has espe-

---

[4] *Parties and Politics in America* (Ithaca, N.Y.: Cornell University Press, 1960), p. 28.

cially plagued the student of comparative politics.[5] Many European countries have compulsory registration or draw up their voting registers from records kept by the police, to whom every change of residence has to be reported. By contrast, registration in the United States is entirely voluntary. Yet even here, a system of permanent or of biennial registration will place more people on the eligible lists than one where each person must register anew for every election.

Although failure to register is probably the most important single cause of nonvoting,[6] it does not follow that a large registration, which is the precondition for a high rate of turnout, does of itself assure it. In fact, the registration, under a permissive system, of a large number of legally eligible voters can well result in a lower turnout rate than a low registration under an inconvenient and more exacting system, where the act of registration is itself a test of the motivation to vote. Some localities with high registration have had chronically low turnouts of registered voters.[7]

By relying on turnout rates based on the proportion of *registered voters* who cast ballots, one can eliminate some of the factors that contaminate the raw-turnout figure, but only by introducing other distorting elements. How many registrants will vote depends in part on the ease with which the administrative barriers to registration are surmounted. Turnout among the registered is thereby less useful as a measure of motivation.

---

[5] See for example Stein Rokkan and Angus Campbell, "The Participation of Citizens in Political Life: Norway and the United States," *International Social Science Journal*, XII (1960), pp. 68–99; and V. O. Key, *Politics, Parties, and Pressure Groups* (New York: Thomas Y. Crowell, 1958). The latter estimates that "raw" turnout rates for the United States would have to be raised by about 6 or 7 percentage points to make them comparable with Western Europe.

[6] Charles E. Merriam and Harold F. Gosnell, *Non-Voting: Causes and Methods of Control* (Chicago: The University of Chicago Press, 1924), p. 37; and Munro Miller, "The Waukegan Study of Voter Turnout Prediction," *Public Opinion Quarterly*, XVI (Fall 1952), pp. 381–98.

[7] A discussion, though a rather dated one, of the relationship between registration and turnout can be found in Joseph P. Harris, *The Registration of Voters in the United States* (Washington, D.C.: The Brookings Institution, 1929), ch. 4.

Over a quarter of a century ago, Herbert Tingsten considered the matter and concluded that, as regards the United States, "a comparison between the number of voters and the number of persons entered on the voting lists . . . will throw no light on the problems of electoral participation in its proper sense."[8] Even area-by-area comparisons of turnout among registered voters can lead to erroneous conclusions and to invalid theories based on them.

One can, however, use the sample survey to investigate directly the reasons that keep individuals from voting. This method involves two basic problems. The first is the problem of sampling nonvoters. The University of Michigan Research Center team, a group with an unusual amount of experience in election surveys, sees the underreporting of the amount of nonvoting in their surveys as unavoidable, the combined effect of four sources of error inherent in the survey procedure:

> (1) the exclusion from the universe sampled of certain categories of persons who do not usually participate in the electoral process — i.e., those residing in institutions and the "floating" population, with no fixed residence or in transit at the time of the election;
>
> (2) the throwing out of some votes because of invalid ballots or improper operation of voting machines;
>
> (3) the greater difficulty of obtaining interviews with nonvoters compared with voters; and
>
> (4) the apparent reluctance of some nonvoters to admit having defaulted in the exercise of their citizen obligation.[9]

Thus the national survey conducted by the Center in 1964 indicated a nonvoting rate of 25 per cent,[10] whereas calculations based on official election figures and population estimates yielded

---

[8] Herbert Tingsten, *Political Behavior: Studies in Election Statistics* (Totowa, N.J.: The Bedminster Press, 1963), p. 30. (First published in 1939.)

[9] Angus Campbell *et al.*, *The American Voter* (New York: John Wiley & Sons, 1960), pp. 90 ff.

[10] Survey Research Center Report, *op. cit.*

a figure of nearly 40 per cent. The estimate is off by about a third.

The second problem concerns the failure of most studies that analyze the causes of nonvoting and voting to maintain the distinction between persons who are fully qualified registered voters and those who are not. If the vast majority of nonvoters in a national election are in fact not registered, the analysis of campaign influences on voting (after registration closes) can yield spurious results. A table in Merriam and Gosnell's pioneering study of nonvoting in the 1923 Chicago mayoralty election reveals that many of the non-registrants cited their failure to meet residence requirements and similar factors as reasons for not voting, reasons that could not possibly apply to those registered.[11] Why, in the light of this, the subsequent analysis of reasons given for nonvoting should contain no separate breakdowns, and the two groups should be always lumped together, is therefore a mystery. Most analyses of nonvoting based on population samples have likewise made no attempt to eliminate the spurious responses of those not registered.

Our investigation of influences presumed to be operating on election day was based on a sample of fully qualified voters, drawn directly from registration lists. Hence its picture of the nonvoter differs in certain respects from that painted in many other studies.

The Case of the Disappearing Nonvoter

Our California sample was designed with the expectation, reasonable in the light of past experience, that about one third of all votes might be cast after 4:00 P.M. and that less than 90 per cent of those registered would vote. On this expectation, the sample drawn from registration lists posted at 4:00 P.M. — with names of all those who had already voted crossed off — should have yielded interviews with about one nonvoter for every three late voters. Sixty per cent would have voted early (by 4:00 P.M.), with the remaining 40 per cent splitting into nonvoters and late voters at a ratio of 1 to 3 or better:

---

[11] *Op. cit.*, p. 37.

All voters		90%
Before 4:00 P.M.	60%	
Late voters	30%	
Nonvoters		10%
All registered		100%

As interviewing progressed, however, admitted nonvoters among this sample of registered voters turned out to be practically nonexistent, accounting for less than 3 per cent of completed interviews. The situation in Ohio was roughly similar.[12]

In seeking to account for the dearth of nonvoters, we could immediately absolve our sampling procedures. The proportion of names crossed off the registration lists in the California precincts as having voted by 4:00 P.M. turned out to be about 65 per cent. Turnout among registered voters, as calculated from the sign-in rosters, was 86 per cent. Even allowing for some errors, random selection should have produced an ample supply of nonvoters, actually nearer a 1-to-2 than a 1-to-3 ratio.

There was always the possibility that our techniques might be at fault, that nonvoters were somehow evading our interviewers or were falsely stating that they had voted when they had not. There was also the chance that the precinct lists were in some way inaccurate and greatly exaggerated the actual amount of nonvoting. We accordingly instituted a special procedure for checking on alleged nonvoters. In the East Bay area we secured pertinent information on 351 nonvoters, roughly 30 per cent of all nonvoters on the registration lists in the sample precincts. In Ohio we have information on attempts to contact 119 nonvoters, amounting to 26 per cent of nonvoters on the lists in the Greater Cleveland precincts. Our search for the elusive

[12] This experience conforms to that reported by other investigators. Mendelsohn, in telephone interviews with 1,724 registered California voters, found 35 who had not voted — about 2 per cent (*op. cit.*). Fuchs, who likewise sampled registration lists for his telephone survey of three West Coast cities, found a nonvoting rate of 4 per cent. See Douglas A. Fuchs, "Election-Day Radio-Television and Western Voting," *Public Opinion Quarterly*, XXX (Summer 1966), p. 233. Still another study conducted under the direction of Nathan Maccoby found too few nonvoters to make any thorough analysis.

nonvoter, though minimal in terms of its yield of additional interviews, provides some assurance that we were dealing with a real phenomenon. The large number of attempted contacts also gave us some serendipitous insights into nonvoting and its causes.

Our interviewers encountered four persons in California and three in Ohio who claimed to have voted though their signatures could not be located on the sign-in rosters. Thus, among a total of twenty-nine persons identified as nonvoters in the two states, seven claimed to have voted whose signatures we were unable to locate on the rosters. This figure of 24 per cent falls within one percentage point of a previous finding by Miller.[13] Nevertheless, we cannot automatically draw the conclusion that all seven were patently lying. Signatures on rosters are sometimes hard to decipher and easy to overlook. Some may have signed their married names and election workers who knew them accepted this discrepancy with the registration list. An occasional voter could likewise have signed the wrong roster or voted in a precinct other than the one sampled. Because we could not be certain in each case whether or not the claim was valid, these interviews were not included in our analysis of nonvoters.

What was this mystery of the disappearing nonvoter? It soon became clear that a considerable number of nonvoters (defined as registered voters who failed to vote) were in actuality spurious nonvoters. At least 71 per cent of the nonvoters in the original California sample[14] and 59 per cent of those in Ohio, so our

---

[13] *Op. cit.*, p. 137. The similarity between his and our figure is all the more striking because Miller's sample, unlike ours, was not confined to persons registered. On attitude items that distinguished "honest voters" from "liars," the latter were more like voters but did not differ from other *non*voters on socio-economic indicators. In his telephone survey, Mendelsohn (*op. cit.*) found only one of six nonvoters willing to acknowledge his failure to vote. Another telephone survey found a similarly high proportion of prevaricators among eighty-two nonvoters. See Douglas A. Fuchs, "Does TV Election News Affect Votes?" *Columbia Journalism Review*, IV (Fall 1965), p. 40.

[14] An additional 117 names of persons whom the lists indicated to be nonvoters were added to the California sample to determine reasons for nonvoting. The estimate of the number moved and died is based on the original sample alone.

interviewers found, had either moved out of the district or died.[15] For this category the nonvoter label was simply a result of their names still appearing on the registration lists in precincts where they no longer resided. The same inaccuracies that result in the inflation of nonvoting among registered voters also result in spuriously high registration figures.[16]

To correct the very considerable exaggeration of the actual amount of nonvoting among registered voters, we subtracted from the number of alleged nonvoters *and* from the number of registered voters all cases where we were able to ascertain *from members of the family or from neighbors* that the person had died or moved out of the precinct. The correction was made with the utmost conservatism. Whenever an interviewer failed to make a contact but could not ascertain the reason for it, the person was assumed to be alive, present, and theoretically able to vote, no matter how many unsuccessful callbacks. When so corrected, the proportion of nonvoters among those registered dropped to 4 per cent in California and to 7 per cent in Ohio.

Real Nonvoting

Relative to Ohio, nonvoting in California now appears even lower than it did before the correction, indicating a higher turnout among registrants in the state where election broadcasts could be heard. The corrected California nonvoting rate of 4

---

[15] Rademaker, in the previously cited study, sought interviews with 213 nonvoters in Oregon and found "spurious nonvoting" to account for about 50 per cent of all nonvoting.

[16] In this connection, see the recent article of Charles G. Bell and William Buchanan, "Reliable and Unreliable Respondents: Party Registration and Prestige Pressure," *Western Political Quarterly*, XIX (March 1966), pp. 37–43, in which the authors found (1) that the names of every third respondent who, in a survey, claimed to be registered could not be located on the roster, but also (2) that the proportion of confirmed registrations among respondents was at least 10 per cent below the official figure. The apparent contradiction is resolved when we consider three factors: the inflation of estimates based on voting rosters, inaccuracies in these rosters — particularly in areas where residential mobility is high — and a much smaller proportion of normal errors by respondents who falsely believe themselves registered at their present address when in fact they are reported elsewhere or have been struck off the rolls.

per cent represents the absolute upper limit within which broadcast-induced late-election-day slack could have occurred.

The correction also makes possible a more accurate estimate of the actual amount of nonvoting among the registrants of the two major parties. When the uncorrected figures are used, nonvoting in California appears to have been more frequent among Democrats, suggesting that the election broadcasts, if responsible for most nonvoting, benefited Goldwater and the candidates running with him on the Republican ticket. This conclusion, however, is refuted by the corrected figures, which indicate slightly less nonvoting among Democrats rather than among Republicans (Table 4.1). Instead of an indirect underdog effect, there may therefore have been a mild indirect bandwagon effect in favor of Johnson and the Democratic ticket. Actually, the high turnout in East Bay, compared with Cleveland, dampens our enthusiasm for either interpretation.

Precinct-by-precinct examination of the uncorrected turnout by registered voters indicates consistently higher electoral participation in the solidly Republican precints. Turnout in Democratic and swing precincts was more variable and on the average lower. These differences among precincts reflect socio-economic rather than political factors, inasmuch as the turnout among Republicans and Democrats in the same precinct was essentially similar, and the differences in rates among the types of precincts (Democratic, Republican, and swing) were clearly greater than those between all registered Republicans and Democrats.

The importance of socio-economic indicators, as compared with political ones, is further underlined when spurious nonvoting is examined on a precinct-by-precinct basis. The inflation of what appears as nonvoting, due to failure to clean up registration lists, is greatest in areas of high residential mobility— in this instance, the heavily Democratic precincts in Negro residential areas. In the Republican precincts, with their older and more established populations, a significant amount of nonvoting reflects the higher crude mortality rate. We can be fairly certain that the "dead souls" carried on registration lists do not indeed vote. However, the impact of higher mobility in the

Table 4.1 Nonvoting Among Registered Voters in California and Ohio Sample Precincts by Party Registration

Party Registration	*Registered*				*Failed to Vote*		*Nonvoters Moved or Died*		*Corrected (Actual) Proportion Nonvoters*	
	California		*Ohio*		*California*	*Ohio*	*California*	*Ohio*	*California*	*Ohio*
	N	%	N	%	%	%	%	%	%	%
Republicans	3977	48	749	25	13	12	65	59	5	5
Democrats	3967	48	763	26	15	11	77	54	4	6
Other or "declined to state"	323	4	1443	49	20	20	74	61	7	9
All registrants	8267	100	2955	100	14	16	71	59	4	7

Democratic precincts on the total Democratic vote cannot be accurately assessed without investigating whether the persons changing residence voted in the districts to which they moved, or whether they were, in effect, disenfranchised.

The elimination of evidently spurious nonvoters left us with 143 cases in California and 49 in Ohio. Table 4.2 gives some indication of the operational problems encountered in seeking interviews with genuine nonvoters, about one out of five of whom refused to be interviewed. About two fifths in California and about one fifth in Ohio managed to elude our interviewers for reasons they could not ascertain. Some of the not-at-homes probably belonged to the transient population, and some may have moved or died. Unfortunately we were not tooled to pursue this line of investigation to its full conclusion.

Despite the less-than-full accounting for every nonvoter, we can nevertheless establish physical difficulties as a major cause of genuine nonvoting among registered voters. We found a number of persons who evidently were kept from voting because they had been ill at home or in the hospital, or because they had been away from their city of residence on election day. Though it was not possible to ascertain whether they would have voted had their circumstances been different, they had obviously not been dissuaded from voting by broadcasts of early returns. With the elimination of these persons, the range within

Table 4.2 Reasons for Nonvoting Among Actual Nonvoters

Reason	*California*		*Ohio*	
	N	%	N	%
Physical difficulty (i.e., ill or out of town, etc.)	42	29	20	41
Abstention (i.e., low interest, discouragement, etc.)	8	6	7	14
Not at home	58	41	9	18
Refused interview	31	22	10	20
Claimed to have voted	4	3	3	6
	143	101*	49	99*

*Due to rounding.

which the broadcasts could have contributed to slack is reduced by at least another third or more. In California the maximum number of nonvoters who could have been responding to returns lies somewhere between 2 and 3 per cent of those registered.[17]

The Registered Nonvoter and the Broadcasts

Interviews were completed with only twelve admitted nonvoters in California and with ten in Ohio. Five of the twelve in California had heard nothing about how the race was going before polls closed. They had little interest in the election or its outcome, and, whatever the reason for their nonvoting, it could not have had anything to do with election broadcasts, which they neither saw themselves nor were told about by others. Of the seven remaining who had been exposed to returns before polls closed,

—four did not vote because they had been ill, and three of these were still bedridden at the time of the interview;

—one said he had long before decided not to vote, as neither of the two candidates offered an attractive alternative;

—one stated vaguely and without referring to the broadcasts at any time that he had not been able to vote in the morning and then was kept from voting later in the day by pressing business (He expressed neither much interest in the election nor a commitment to voting.);

—one, a strong Goldwater partisan, had intended to vote but did not after he learned from election broadcasts that the race had already been decided and that his vote would be "useless."

The last was the one case of nonvoting in response to election news we were able to discover.

Two of ten nonvoters interviewed in Cleveland claimed to have

---

[17] Both Merriam and Gosnell (*op. cit.*, p. 37) and Rademaker (*op. cit.*) present data that similarly highlight the importance of physical reasons as a major cause of nonvoting among registered voters.

heard returns before polls closed. Since the network coverage of the election did not begin until a half hour after the end of balloting in that state, any estimates of the outcome these nonvoters heard must have been based either on very scattered returns or on reports of turnout in different areas and the deductions therefrom. In any event, both these nonvoters were kept away from the polls by illness, and not by what they may have heard. The explanations given by the other eight in Ohio had a quality very similar to those given by nonvoters in California.

Some characteristics found among these California nonvoters, too small for meaningful statistical comparisons, are nevertheless of interest, because they tend to characterize registered nonvoters everywhere. The California group contained a high concentration of older people with little education, i.e., non-graduates from high school who were over fifty-five years old. Nonvoters generally exhibited less involvement both in the outcome of the election and in the campaign that led up to it. Thus, exactly half of them reported that they had taken little or no interest in the campaign, a response given by only one out of six of the voters. Most nonvoters had weak partisan commitments. Only two out of twelve stated a clear preference for one of the presidential candidates over the other, and, among those who saw "little difference," the main reason was that neither candidate appeared "particularly good" rather than that both were highly qualified. On our criterion of involvement in the election, 55 per cent of the late voters thought that "who won made a good deal of difference" *and* that this election was "more important than most elections," but only one nonvoter expressed himself this strongly. He was kept from voting by a *pre*-election-night hangover, and he might have picked himself up and gone to vote had the returns indicated an extremely close race in which his vote might have made a difference.

The marginal involvement of most nonvoters in the electoral contest implies that they would have been especially open to the potentially dissuasive influence, or to other influences, from the early returns. However, the likelihood that they would vote in any case is small to begin with. In addition, our data show that this same marginal involvement kept most from tuning in to the election broadcasts at a time when they could still have gone to the polls. They began to follow returns, on the average, later than those who voted. These two observations provide no grounds for a conclusion that the early availability of returns via election broadcasts deterred more than a few. Our one documented case of late-election-day slack represents the only instance of a person who would have gone to the polls if it had not been for the reports of the overwhelming Johnson landslide.

All respondents, including nonvoters, were also asked whether on election day they had participated in or been the target of informal or formal electioneering activity and so might have been indirectly influenced by the returns. Seven California nonvoters reported that others had urged them to be sure to vote, urgings that evidently remained ineffective. When asked specifically whether any of these attempts at persuasion made mention of election returns, no nonvoter had any recollection that they did. However, one California nonvoter replied affirmatively to the query, "Did anyone suggest to you on election day that it was no longer important whether or not you voted?" Yet, given what this nonvoter revealed of his orientation in other parts of the interview, we doubt that the suggestion had any greater influence on him than on ten others who, although similarly advised, went to vote none the less.

Considering the decisive lead Johnson held in the returns, the 1964 presidential election maximized the possibility that voters might respond to the early returns by staying away from the polls. The one pro-Goldwater voter who lost all interest in voting, because he became disgusted and demoralized, represents a loss of about one third of one per cent of the potential vote among the California sample. Had there been any sizeable amount of late-election-day slack, more evidence of its existence should have turned up in this study. To estimate the precise amount of slack throughout the state or nation from a single instance would clearly be unwarranted, but we can conclude that it must have been extremely limited. The evidence to be presented in the next chapter suggests, moreover, that the few cases of slack were more than offset by influences that moved potential nonvoters everywhere in the direction of voting.

Broader Implications

Our observations on nonvoting have implications that extend beyond these particulars. The first is methodological. If so large a number of registered voters are in fact mere names on registration lists, then any comparisons of voter turnout based on the proportion of registered voters who vote must incorporate methods for correcting whatever bias this spurious nonvoting may create. The problem is not unique to the analysis of American voting statistics. "If it were possible, when calculating the number of abstentions," George Dupeux writes in a discussion of electoral participation in France, "to take into account the citizens who are old enough to vote but are unable to do so because their names are not on the rolls, the percentage of abstentions would be found to be higher. Conversely, if the electoral rolls are not kept up to date, if the names of electors who die or change their domicile are not deleted, the actual proportion of abstentions is obviously lower than that shown by the official statistics. A recent experiment carried out in a number of towns, chiefly in the south of France, brought to light certain defects or irregularities in the electoral rolls, which give food for thought. A more detailed study of this problem should be undertaken, and it might well be that the differences which are often noted between regions (polling is usually much heavier in the northern than in the southern regions) are due, not to differences in the behavior of citizens, but simply to the greater or lesser efficiency with which the local authorities prepare the rolls."[18]

Most studies on comparative turnout, whether between districts, regions, or countries, acknowledge the possibility of such bias, but they make little attempt to assess its magnitude and direction, or to adjust their figures in the light of it. In this study, as was shown, a correction that took account of the

---

[18] George Dupeux, "The Participation of Citizens in Political Life: France," *International Social Science Journal*, X (1960), p. 40.

greater amount of spurious nonvoting among registered Democrats completely reversed an implication from the uncorrected data. What appeared to be mild evidence for the existence of a slight indirect underdog effect in favor of Goldwater turned out to be more consistent with an indirect bandwagon effect in favor of Johnson. In both instances, however, the evidence was too weak to be conclusive.

On a more substantive level, we surmise that once we account for legal disqualification and physical obstacles to voting, much nonvoting in the United States represents a chronic exclusion from electoral participation rather than fluctuating political interest. Being registered is still the best single indicator that a person will vote.[19]

Also to be considered is the effect of registration practices on the various kinds of nonvoting. The majority of real nonvoters are not and probably never were registered. In California as well as in Ohio, a person who votes in an election is carried on the electoral rolls for another two years. He remains qualified to vote in the district unless he moves or fails to exercise his franchise. The corrected figures for turnout among registered voters indicate that, within the framework set by present registration practices, most of the nonvoting in this group is spurious; the proportion of the registered who go to the polls in a presidential election is near optimum. We have already noted that the rising pitch of a presidential campaign, with its saturation of the mass media, brings to the polls practically every registered voter who is not deterred by some difficulty. In a series of experiments to increase voter turnout, Gosnell showed some thirty years ago that "the proportion of registered citizens who vote (in an aldermanic election) could be increased even in wards where there was no election contest."[20] Persons were persuaded to vote even though ballots could have no effect on the election of a candi-

---

[19] Thomas C. McCormick and J. Richard Wahl, "Predicting Election Turnout: A Test of a Behavior Hypothesis," *American Journal of Sociology*, LXI (July 1955), pp. 39–48. Registered voters in this sample of the population had a turnout rate of 98.5 per cent — 151 out of 154 who were registered.

[20] Gosnell, *op. cit.*, p. 107 f.

date. In these cases, the act of voting served principally as a "ratifying gesture" on the part of people who had somehow committed themselves to vote.

Hence the crucial social-psychological factor is the voter's long-term commitment to participation in the electoral process. The momentary strength and weakness of partisan pressures, or their consistency, plays a role, but studies that fail to inquire into who among their sample are registered are inclined to mistake the consequence for the cause. Thus, the person for whom politics lacks salience does not bother to register. For the same reason, the social groups in which he participates are not apt to reflect homogeneous political norms, but rather a variety of preferences that have no firm social base. While an electoral campaign puts pressure on the politically committed citizen to bring his own views in line with those of his associates, the chronic nonvoter can easily tolerate cross-pressures because he does not intend to vote.

The widening of eligibility and the easing of registration regulations have indirect consequences for turnout. For example, the extension of suffrage rights to all American women was accompanied by a very marked decline in the proportion of "eligibles" casting ballots in presidential elections. The fact that many newly enfranchised ladies failed to vote was as responsible for low electoral turnout in the 1920s as the balmy political climate of that decade. By the same token, the sudden mobilization of legally eligible but previously passive citizens injects an element of potential instability into the political system, especially when party polarization is weak, as it normally is in primaries or off-year elections or in political constituencies where politics are nonpartisan by tradition.

Fluctuations in turnout are most important in primaries, local elections, and referendums, where participation even by registered voters is much lower than in presidential elections. Greater fluctuations of turnout in presidential elections could be brought about by a dramatic increase in registration, particularly if this were the result of revised, more permissive registration procedures. Where those fully qualified to vote encompass a large number of citizens only marginally committed to participation in the electoral process, the impact of specific historical circumstances, including mass-communication events, on turnout is potentially greater. Our findings, which play down the importance of slack, do not justify an out-of-hand rejection of the possibility of quantitatively more significant amounts of slack in elections held under different circumstances.

• 5 •

The Impact on Voting: Bandwagon and Underdog Effects

Did persons who voted after hearing election news cast their ballots differently than they would have had there been no early returns? Did their pre-voting perceptions of the likely outcome influence their decisions in any way?

Before presenting the evidence, we set forth three relevant and familiar propositions about the role of communications in the crystallization of votes:[1]

(1) The closer election day approaches, the greater the proportion of the electorate who have made up their minds how to vote and the less the likelihood that large numbers will change.

(2) The most frequent effect of political communications during an electoral campaign is to reinforce prior convictions rather than to convert voters to new positions.

(3) Voters with weak commitments, who are subject to

---

[1] For the source of these propositions, see among others: Berelson *et al.*, *op. cit.*, especially the appendix; S. M. Lipset *et al.*, "The Psychology of Voting," Ch. 20 in the *Handbook of Social Psychology*, edited by G. Lindzey, Cambridge, Mass.: Addison-Wesley, 1954), II, pp. 1124–75; Klapper, *op. cit.*; and Lang and Lang, *op. cit.*

motivational cross-pressures or in doubt about how to vote or whether to vote at all, are most subject to influence by communications from all sources.

As to the potential effect of broadcast returns, the following inferences can now be drawn: The first proposition suggests that there would normally be very few vote switches on election day. The second implies that the returns would somehow serve to justify what people had been inclined to do all along. Among registered voters, most of whom are in the habit of voting, the inclination to cast a ballot, and to cast it for the candidate preferred, would be reinforced rather than eroded. And from the third proposition comes the suggestion that the potential for change would be maximized when political polarization is weak or when the floating vote is exceptionally large. On the basis of data from the 1964 election, we can determine whether and how partisans and persons only marginally involved in the election were influenced.

Last-Minute Shifts

We indicated in Chapter 1 that the proportion of Johnson voters among late voters interviewed exceeded considerably the proportion of the Johnson voters within the precincts sampled. In that discussion we were mainly concerned with showing that the heavily pro-Johnson responses of the "late voter" sample accurately reflected the political coloring of the late vote, and was not due to sample bias or response errors. We supposed the higher proportion of Democratic registrants among those voting after 4 P.M. to be a function of the demographic characteristics that determine time of voting. Since the difference found in California between earlier voters and those casting ballots after 4:00 P.M. also turned up in Ohio, we saw no reason to infer that pro-Johnson proclivities of late voters reflected last-minute bandwagon effects specifically attributable to the early election returns.

More detailed breakdowns on the two-party vote among late voters strengthen our reluctance to accept any such inference solely based on time of voting. In the period after 4:00 P.M., the proportions voting for Johnson and for Goldwater fluctuated from one half-hour period to the next, but no over-all trend was apparent. The differences are well within normal sampling fluctuation.[2] Nor was there any patterned shift in the proportions of registered Republicans or Democrats coming to vote as poll closing time neared. Also, voters continued to come out to the polls in about the same proportions in Republican, Democratic, and swing precincts. The distribution of the two-party vote for senator likewise held steady. In other words, the available statistics provide no evidence *either* that, as returns came in, voters were defecting from one party or candidate to the other, *or* that the supporters of one party or candidate mobilized or were dissuaded from voting in disproportionate numbers.

After 4 P.M., the proportion who went to the polls with at least some perception of how the race was going increased considerably as time passed, and the proportion who had become certain by the time they voted increased even more. This does not, however, appear to have had any effect on how they voted. The most striking impression from Table 5.1 is that voters with and without pre-voting preceptions of the race, whether or not they had become certain, split their votes between Goldwater and Johnson in nearly identical proportions. Is the mild and unreliable rise in the Johnson majority (67 per cent) among those voting in the last ninety minutes evidence of a last-minute bandwagon effect? One immediately notes that Johnson fared at least as well (73 per cent) among late-late voters *not exposed* to the broadcasts. The size of the Johnson majority shows no systematic relationship to what people had heard about returns.

Potentially most subject to influence were those voting latest. Eighty persons in the California sample, less than one fourth

---

[2] Douglas Fuchs, "Election-Day Radio-Television and Western Voting," *op. cit.*, presents data based on a much larger sample which support our negative observation. The proportion of the two-party total received by Johnson can be calculated from data in Table 3 of that article. The proportion was 63 per cent among persons voting between 5:00 and 6:00 P.M., and 67 per cent among those voting after 6:00 P.M. Our data show proportions of 66 per cent and 61 per cent respectively.

Table 5.1 Per Cent of Two-Party Presidential Vote for Johnson by Time of Voting and Conclusion from Returns

	Conclusion Drawn		*Voters with*		
Time of Voting	*Johnson Certain*	*Less than Certain*	*Some News before Voting*	*No News before Voting*	*Total Voters*
After 4:00 but by 5:30 P.M.	62	56	59	68	63
After 5:30 but by 6:30 P.M.	55	67	60	61	60
After 6:30 P.M.	68	58	65	73	67
All late voters	61	61	61	66	63
Total late voters*	(111)	(92)	(203)	(121)	(334)

*Persons who did not vote for President or refused to reveal how they voted are not included in the base from which the percentages were derived.

of all late voters, cast ballots between 6:30 and 8:00 P.M. Initially we had intended to treat as "late-late voters" only persons who went to the polls in the last hour of balloting; but voting in most of the precincts sampled had by this time been reduced to a trickle, following a rush that reached its peak shortly before 6:00 P.M. In some precincts, the vote cast in the last hour amounted to less than 1 per cent of the total vote. It was limited to a few stragglers who wandered in as officials sat waiting to close, to count the vote, and go home. (After all, most precinct workers had also learned, long before their job of counting votes had begun, that the election was already over.) Including those who voted after 6:30 P.M. in the late-late vote provided us with a larger pool of persons, all of whom had had about equal opportunity to hear *conclusive* returns before voting.

The slack in the vote during the last hour might suggest that:

(1) the usual last-minute electioneering drive did not develop in 1964;

(2) those never highly motivated to vote in the first place were therefore left free not to vote; and

(3) they were not pressured to go to the polls, as they might have been in a close election.

This line of argument, though somewhat involved, is certainly plausible. The possibility it raises is not ruled out by our prior finding that hardly anyone had been actively dissuaded by the returns, but rests on the expectation that the number with weak political commitments who vote is usually greatest among those voting last.

To begin with, we failed to obtain any testimony from interviews with late voters that even one of them had been brought to the polls by election workers, or that he had been induced to cast a ballot in response to personal pressure and against his own inclination. With regard to political interest and involvement in the outcome of the election, the late-late voters were very much like those who cast ballots between 4:00 and 6:30 P.M. There were no significant differences in the amount of attention each group had paid to the campaign, in the importance each gave to the election and to who won, in their confidence in the efficacy of citizen participation in the electoral process, or in a number of other politically relevant characteristics.

These findings are highly inconclusive, as negative findings usually are. Once again, the observations in Ohio, where election broadcasts could not be heard, help evaluate the likelihood that an indirect broadcast effect, mediated through the default of party workers, was responsible for the small vote during the last hour in California. There was no decline of political interest and involvement among last-minute voters in Ohio either. In other words, if no *last-minute* effort to pull voters to the polls materialized in California in 1964, this was not a peculiarity of the state where early network returns were heard. Failure to electioneer more actively may reflect a shared expectation, already widespread before returns began coming in, that the race would not be at all close — that it was over before it had even begun. In any event, the drive by the organization to get out the vote is usually more closely linked to local contests than it is to the contest for the presidency. Most of this work must have taken place earlier in the day and was therefore independent of what the returns showed.

The shortened work day, the higher proportion of women who work away from home, the legal obligation of employers to give time off to vote, and other developments have weakened what once was a rather marked difference in the status of those voting early and those voting late. Our group of late-late voters was made up largely of people who stopped by to vote on their way home from work. It contained a somewhat disproportionate number of men, of the well-to-do, and of persons who had attended college. Though none of these contrasts are striking, they may help clarify the reasons behind what we first thought to be a chance variation in the political characteristics of those voting in the different time periods after 4:00 P.M. They are particularly noteworthy since this variation between characteristics of the late vote and the late-late vote turned up in Cleveland as well.

To explain: The late-late vote in California contained a disproportionately large number of self-styled independents and of persons who reported that, in past elections, they had voted about "equally often" for the two major parties. Many of these were former Rockefeller supporters (Table 5.2). Of the registered Republicans casting ballots in the last ninety minutes the polls were open, 85 per cent gave evidence of some conflict — that is, they said they had voted for Rockefeller in the primary

Table 5.2 Anti-Goldwater Republicans by Time of Voting

Time of Voting	*Voted for Rockefeller in Primary*		*Registered Republicans*				*All Others*		*Total Voters*
			"In Conflict"		*Regulars*				
	N	%	N	%	N	%	N	%	N
After 4:00 but by 5:30 P.M.	25	17	29	20	33	23	82	57	144
After 5:30 but by 6:30 P.M.	21	17	36	29	16	13	73	58	125
After 6:30 P.M.	20	25	28	35	5	6	47	59	80
Total responses*	66		93		54		202		349

*Does not include nonvoters and persons on whom sufficient information was not obtained.

or, reluctant to say for whom they voted, indicated they finally voted for someone they had *not* favored before the party nominating conventions.

Anti-Goldwater Republicans throughout the nation contributed heavily to the floating vote that gave Johnson his top-heavy majority in the 1964 election. Their high representation among the late-late vote makes it important for us to ask how hearing returns might have influenced this category of voters to resolve whatever conflict they experienced between loyalty to the Republican party and their disinclination to support its candidate. Would such a "Republican-in-conflict" vote for Goldwater once he discovered a vote for Johnson could no longer affect the outcome of the presidential race, but only the size of the majority? Or, might the evident Democratic landslide provide the final justification for voting against Goldwater, since one vote could not possibly account for the defeat of one's party?

Sixty-six Republicans who had cast ballots for Rockefeller in the California primary split their presidential vote 5 to 3 in favor of Johnson. However, among the twenty who cast their vote in the last ninety minutes of voting, sixteen voted for Johnson. On the face of it, this may look like a bandwagon effect of some magnitude. We have, however, no evidence that any of these Republicans voting for Johnson deferred voting to see how Goldwater was doing, or that they might have shifted if it seemed the Republican stood a chance of capturing the White House. Their voting histories suggest that they were somewhat more independent and deliberative than the average voter. Their conflict derived from political considerations, and if they reacted to the remote chance that Goldwater might win, they did so before they heard any election news. Among Rockefeller voters we could establish no linkage between exposure to returns and the decision either to vote Democratic or to stick with the G.O.P. Most such decisions were made before election day.

Election Day Decisions

What decisions did late voters make on election day? Everyone was explicitly questioned about whether he had made *any* kind of decision relevant to his vote on election day itself. There appeared no great reluctance on the part of persons to admit that they had made such decisions. A slightly smaller proportion of Californians (9 per cent) than Ohioans (16 per cent) mentioned one or more decisions, and an identical 2 per cent in each state reported decisions relevant to their vote for president (Table 5.3). Slightly more Californians than Ohioans reported a decision about the senatorial contest. The major difference between the two areas was in the number of decisions relating to local matters, on which the opportunity to hear returns clearly had no bearing.

Actually, the majority of all decisions in both states related to local contests and propositions, and very few concerned the presidency. This finding is altogether plausible, since the contest for the top of the ticket always receives much more attention in the mass media and generates the greatest partisan interest. Hence the number of voters who fail to reach a firm decision on the presidency before election day is, under most circumstances, quite small, with those who have no real intention to vote usually remaining undecided longest. As a rule, there is much less pressure to make an early decision with regard to local races, or on questions and propositions. Thus, some persons find themselves confronted, on election day, with the need to make an immediate decision on a candidate or an issue to which they have given only minimal thought beforehand.

Past studies furthermore tell us that high interest in a political campaign usually goes together with strong partisanship and

Table 5.3 Vote Decisions Made on Election Day

Decision Regarding	*California (N = 352)*		*Ohio (N = 106)*	
	N	%	N	%
Presidency	7	2	2	2
Senate race	8	2	1	1
Local matters	22	6	15	14
Total decisions made*	32	9	17	16

*Some respondents reported decision on more than one level.

an early vote decision.[3] Accordingly, the person who defers his decision on how to vote for president until election day would most often be a person who has less than the usual interest in the campaign and, by the same token, is even less concerned about local contests, referendums, and so forth. Many of these voters are unlikely to exercise the full range of choices on their ballots or, if they do, are guided mainly by party labels or by "sample ballots" printed up by local politicians. If this is true, their vote, especially on local matters, is not apt to involve a "decision" in the sense of deliberative thought.

By contrast, the votes of persons who are concerned about local matters are more likely to involve a definite decision, even if it is not made until election day. These persons are highly likely, because of their greater involvement in politics generally, to have decided how to vote for the top offices some time before. Hence, one would expect to find a difference between the type of voter apt to make a last-minute decision on a major office and the type of voter apt to come to a last-minute decision on local matters.

Interest in the campaign was indeed lowest among persons whose election day decisions related to the presidency. Apparently the difference between the alternatives did not appear to them very salient. This lack of strong interest in the campaign and in the election also extended to election returns. On the other hand, persons whose election day decisions concerned local matters more often had pre-voting perceptions of the outcome of the presidential race, and more of them had, on the basis of these perceptions, become certain of who would win (Table 5.4).

It does not appear, therefore, that pre-voting perceptions had a great influence on the last-minute presidential decisions reported by late voters. Not only is the total number of decisions on all matters small, but one notes that persons who made last-minute decisions about the national contest were less likely to have come to any definitive conclusions, based on returns, on how the presidential race was coming out. Parenthetically, it

---

[3] Berelson *et al.*, *op cit.*

Table 5.4 Conclusions from Early Returns by Those Making Decisions on Election Day (California Only)

	Decision Regarding:							
Conclusion Drawn	*Presidency*		*Senate Race*		*Local Matters*		*No Decision*	
	N	%	N	%	N	%	N	%
Johnson, certain	1	25	1	17	11	65	106	56
Johnson, probably	3	75	3	50	5	29	28	15
No conclusion, Goldwater ahead, etc.	0	—	2	33	1	6	57	30
All exposed to returns	4	100	6	100	17	100	191	101†
All late voters and nonvoters*	7		8		22		320	
% of total "certain"		14		13		50		33
% of total exposed to returns		57		75		77		60
% of total with "great deal of interest" in campaign		43		87		82		72

*Includes only respondents on whom complete information was obtained.
†Due to rounding.

may be pointed out that none of those reporting a decision with regard to the Senate was among the thirty-five who had heard Senate returns before voting.

Asked about the specific content of his decisions, not a single late voter in either state reported having *switched* from one candidate to another, with regard to either the race for president or that for United States senator. All but one of eighteen decisions (California *and* Ohio) relevant to these two offices represent vote crystallizations by persons who had been seriously thinking of *not* voting for a particular candidate, i.e., sitting out the race, but who on election day decided finally to cast a ballot. The single exception was a registered Democrat in California who had been toying with the idea of withholding a vote from Salinger; on election day this intent was firmed up.[4]

To the extent that one can extrapolate from seven decisions with regard to the presidency, Goldwater may have benefited more from the last-minute crystallizations among the California electorate than did Johnson. Five persons decided to vote for the Arizona senator after all, one additional vote went for Johnson, and the seventh crystallizer was an anti-Goldwater Republican who refused to say for whom he finally cast his presidential ballot.

Are these particular decisions evidence for a *direct* underdog effect in response to early election returns? No firm conclusion can be reached by comparing the decisions of the four persons with pre-voting perceptions and the three without such. A detailed look at the four, whose decisions may have had been influenced by early returns, does point up the variety of possible reactions to hearing results before voting and the complex judgmental processes involved. All four saw Johnson as clearly ahead; one was certain that he would win and the others, though less than certain, believed he would most probably win.

The decision of the one person who had become certain entailed a pro-Goldwater crystallization by a Republican-in-con-

---

[4] The one case of slack reported in Chapter 4, it will be recalled, also represents a decision not to vote.

flict, who had had serious prior doubts about the wisdom of his party's nominating a conservative and who now decided to vote for him nevertheless. The crystallization was not a response to returns from the presidential race, however, but to early returns from the Senate race. These led the respondent to the conclusion that Murphy, whom he had expected to lose in a close race, stood a real chance of defeating Salinger. He became more eager to vote and so to help nail down the Murphy victory. In the course of this, he also decided to cast a vote for Goldwater — perhaps because the race was already decided and his vote could make no difference.

Of the three other election-day deciders who thought Johnson would probably win but had not yet become certain, two likewise resulted in crystallization of Goldwater votes. In neither case could we find any relationship between the knowledge of how the race for president was going and the decision to vote for Goldwater. One of these crystallizers was a registered Democrat, who normally voted Democrat and therefore needed time for his antipathy toward Johnson to overcome his party loyalty. The other was a registered Republican-in-conflict, who had *not* been for Goldwater until after he was nominated. Upon learning that Johnson would probably win, he allegedly became less eager to vote for president. Yet, he had strong partisan commitments with regard to the Senate race; his decision to vote for Goldwater once again seemed to have more to do with what he heard about the Senate race than about presidential returns. He saw Salinger running more strongly than he had expected, and, while this involved no decision, it made him definitely more eager to cast his vote for Murphy as the Senate race still hung in doubt. Again the Senate race seems to have provided the stronger motivation, inasmuch as this person, though he voted for Goldwater, did so without any enthusiasm.

These brief profiles offer a picture of the last-minute decider who had been hearing returns. The picture is not in line with that usually drawn in the literature. The last-minute deciders exhibited some degree of independence. Their motives were often complex, involving some deliberation over alternatives, and they were responding to many events other than the impending Johnson landslide. The votes of those who heard returns clearly did not crystallize out of a naive or simple desire to go with the winner, or from mere sympathy for the loser, especially since the returns brought no surprises. By contrast, the election day deciders who fit more closely the image of the waverer with only marginal interest in voting were late voters who had *not* heard returns prior to voting. This group, while perhaps potentially more susceptible to direct influence from returns, would be less likely to be on the lookout for them, and to this extent would be more insulated from any possible influence.

The Crystallization of Votes

Did knowledge of early returns, in general, have the effect of overcoming whatever prior reservations a respondent had about voting, or about voting for every office? Or, were such crystallizations primarily a response to the momentum a campaign always seems to gather in its closing days?

Every late voter was queried on whether or not he had "seriously considered at any time during the campaign" any one, or combination, of the following alternatives:

(1) not voting at all,

(2) voting without casting a ballot for president, and

(3) voting without casting a ballot for senator.

A person answering "yes" to any of these alternatives was then asked whether he had still been seriously considering this particular form of abstention on election day itself.

Nearly one out of every five late voters[5] in California replied that he had seriously entertained one or more of these alternatives; in Ohio, one out of six likewise responded affirmatively (Table 5.5). Because the contest for presidency normally overshadows all other contests in the same election, it is not surprising that most of those seriously thinking about not voting at all had been responding mainly to the choice — or to what they saw as a lack of choice — for president. In fact, more than half

[5] The question was not asked of nonvoters.

Table 5.5 Late Voters who Considered Not Voting Before or on Election Day

	Potential Abstainers					
Consideration	*Before Election Day Seriously Considered*		*On Election Day Still Seriously Considered*		*On Election Day Carried Out Intent**	
CALIFORNIA	N	%	N	%	N	%
Not voting at all	25		6		0	
Not voting for president	37		12		3	
Not voting for senator	21		8		6	
Some form of abstention†	68	19	23	6	9	3
Never considered non-voting	284	81	329	94	343	97
Total voters	352	100	352	100	352	100
OHIO	N	%	N	%	N	%
Not voting at all	11		0		0	
Not voting for president	9		2		2	
Not voting for senator	3		2		2	
Some form of abstention†	18	17	4	4	4	4
Never considered non-voting	88	83	102	96	102	96
Total voters	106	100	106	100	106	100

*These questions were not asked of nonvoters, and therefore the possible effect of the network returns on actual total abstentions cannot be inferred from this table but only from other data.

†Some entertained more than one form of abstention, i.e., sixty-eight persons in California gave a total of 83 affirmative replies, and 18 persons in Ohio gave a total of 23 affirmative replies.

of the twenty-five who said they had entertained thoughts of "not voting at all" had also entertained the alternative of voting without casting a ballot for president. Since our first question was about "not voting at all," it is even possible that some respondents were answering this only with regard to the presidency, and that they may have judged the next question to be redundant. Only one respondent linked "not voting at all" with not voting for senator, and one actually considered all three possibilities, at least so he stated.

Since more of the late voters had seriously deliberated about the possibility of not voting for president than about not voting for senator, this group of potential nonvoters and abstainers also contains, as one would infer, an unusually large proportion who said the candidate for whom they ultimately voted had not been their first choice prior to the party nominating conventions. These observations are pretty much replicated in Ohio. They point to the focal function of the presidential contest in mobilizing the vote.

In both states, a large majority of those who had thought of abstaining reported that they had reached a firm decision to vote and vote for all offices *before* election day. But among those who continued to entertain such thoughts on election day, those weighing an abstention in the presidential voting still outnumbered those who thought they might sit out the Senate race. Only when it came to carrying through on these thoughts were there fewer persons not voting for president than for senator. Of thirty-seven persons who had at some time considered not voting for president, only three ended up not marking their presidential ballot, but six out of twenty-one persons passed up the opportunity to vote for senator. In Ohio also, persons who had thought about not voting for senator were more likely to follow through than persons who considered not voting for president. It would appear that anyone inclined to vote cannot, without some unease, refrain from voting for the highest office — as the larger number of votes usually cast for the top office testifies.

As regards the resolution of doubts about voting, there is one difference between California and Ohio: Every Ohio late voter who, on election day, was still considering not voting for some office did, in fact, abstain; whereas in California *half* of those who considered abstaining either for president or senator ended up voting. This corroborates our previous hunch that returns may have actually helped persuade people to vote, even if they did so with less enthusiasm than they might otherwise have.

Since concern over the early dissemination of election news centered on the presidential election, let us look closely at its possible influence on fifty-one California late voters who had at some time considered not voting for president — either by itself, or in conjunction with not voting at all or not voting for United States senator. By the time they voted (or could have voted), two out of three (34) had heard something of how the race was going, and two out of five (20) had become certain that Johnson would win (Table 5.6). Three persons ended up by not voting for president; of these, two had heard returns and became certain that Johnson would win. But if becoming certain kept them from voting, it had no such influence on the eighteen others who interpreted what they were exposed to in the same way.

The three persons in California who deliberately abstained from voting for president are interesting political types. Two were nonparty registrants who cast ballots for Murphy. One of these, who identified himself as voting more often Democratic and claimed to have voted for Kennedy in 1960, had not been exposed to the returns; the other denied that what he heard affected his decisions in any way. The third person to abstain was a first-time voter; a registered Democrat, he was strongly anti-Johnson but cast a vote for Salinger. Having become certain before he went to the polls that Johnson would

Table 5.6 Conclusions from Returns by Persons Having Considered Not Voting or Not Voting for President

Conclusion Drawn	*Potential Abstainers*		*Others*	
	N	%	N	%
Johnson, certain	20	59	98	55
Johnson, probably	6	18	30	17
No conclusion, Goldwater ahead, etc.	8	24	51	28
All exposed to returns	34	101†	179	100
All late voters and nonvoters*	51		301	
% of total "Certain"		39		33
% of total Exposed to Returns		67		60

*Includes only respendents on whom complete information was obtained.
†Due to rounding.

win, his prior inclination not to cast a presidential ballot was reinforced. The scattered Senate returns he heard led him to believe that Murphy held a near-decisive edge. This made him more eager to vote for Salinger, whom he wanted to win.[6] As we shall see later in Chapter 6, concern over the outcome of the senate race seems generally to have played a significant part in inhibiting slack among the late voters.

News heard before voting seems not to have dissuaded any potential abstainers from voting, but the attitudinal reaction to this news is a somewhat more sensitive indicator of whether the broadcasts were an impetus toward voting or nonvoting. As shown in Table 5.7, a disproportionate number of persons with doubts about voting for president reported a change of attitude in response to what they had learned. Even more important, these changes were predominantly negative, a majority

Table 5.7 Eagerness to Vote by Persons Having Considered Not Voting or Not Voting for President

	Potential Abstainers							
Attitudinal Reaction	*Considered Abstention on Election Day*		*Firm Decision Before Election Day*		*(1) + (2)*		*Other Late Voters**	
	N	%	N	%	N	%	N	%
More eager	0	0	3	13	3	9	34	18
Less eager	6	55	3	13	9	26	13	7
All changes (more and less eager)	6	55	6	26	12	35	47	25
No attitudinal change	5	45	17	74	22	65	139	75
Total exposed	11	100	23	100	34	100	186	100
All late voters and nonvoters†	17		34		51		301	
% of total exposed		69		66		67		62

*Two nonvoters who became "less eager" are not included.
†Includes only respondents on whom complete information was obtained.

[6] Senate returns were apparently not a factor in the six abstentions from casting a Senate vote; none of the six had heard anything about the Senate race before going to vote.

indicating that they became less eager to vote. Indeed, these fifty-one persons, representing some 14 per cent of late voters sampled, account for just about 40 per cent of all the "less eager" reactions reported by late voters. Why then did all but three eventually end up voting for president? The majority who did (56 per cent) said they cast their vote "against" rather than "for" a candidate, but only one third of all other late voters were so motivated. There apparently is a distinct relationship between this kind of negative orientation — voting against the worse of two candidates — and a tendency toward abstaining from voting for either.

This same negative orientation helps explain the reaction of these people to returns heard. The few who, even on election day, still were not sure they would vote tended to feel even less eager after they had heard the results. Of the eleven who had heard returns, six reported having had a negative reaction; yet all but one of the six voted for president even though they felt less like casting a vote than before.

The large number of potential abstainers who felt less like voting after hearing election returns confirms the general proposition that political communications during a campaign have the greatest impact on persons beset by doubts or who lack a firm intent to begin with. Thus the inclination of potential abstainers to withhold votes seems to have gained support. Why then did so many of them vote nevertheless? Why were there not more abstentions, especially since a vote for president no longer seemed to matter for the outcome? Do these attitudinal reactions have no bearing on behavior, or were they counteracted by other forces that impelled people to vote regardless of how unenthusiastic they felt?

What needs to be taken into account is that most voters, including the vast majority of abstainers, had pretty much committed themselves long before election day to vote for all major offices. Hearing election returns sometimes reactivated the doubts potential abstainers had had about voting. Most of them had construed their sitting out the election as a deliberate act of political protest. If they had had a different choice, they would never have questioned that they should vote. To have abstained from voting would have gone against deep-seated attitudes that were shared by most.

Voting as Collective Behavior

Voting is not just an individual act, but the outcome of a host of interpersonal and mass influences, all of which must be taken into account to explain why people were not dissuaded from going to the polls by what they were able to hear about the outcome. The drive to get out the vote, in particular, sets the context within which any early election news is heard, and the crystallization of votes among the late voters obviously involves something more than a direct response to the election coverage. Election day is merely the climax of an extended campaign — the payoff for all the formal and informal electioneering activities in which the two parties have vied with one another to solicit as much voter support as they can. These other political communications in their totality have the effect of sharpening the perceptions of the electorate and of firming up the intention to vote.

On election day itself, all the mass media — newspapers, radio, and television — seem to join with party officials and precinct workers in a general drive to get out the vote. The networks themselves repeatedly interrupt their coverage of election returns to urge all registered voters, irrespective of party, to be sure to go to the polls. Hearing definitive returns would certainly make one's own vote seem anticlimactic. Yet the mere fact that an election is being held exerts strong pressure for people to go to the polls.

To reconstruct *all* the various influences that helped bring respondents to the polls is manifestly impossible. We nevertheless did make an effort to find out the extent to which late voters in our sample had participated in, and/or themselves been the object of formal and informal electioneering activities on election day. Every respondent in California and Ohio was therefore asked: "As a result of what you had seen or heard in the early returns about the race for president or U.S. senators . . .

did you urge anybody to switch his vote?

did you tell anyone to be sure to vote?

did you suggest to anyone else that it was no longer important whether or not he voted?

Judging from responses, many more late voters and nonvoters in Ohio, where no decisive returns could have been heard prior to the time the polls closed, had urged others to be sure to vote (46 per cent) than in California (21 per cent), where the Johnson victory seemed inevitable long before voting had ended. Very few in either state said that, on election day, they had tried to persuade anyone that he should switch. The question is, as always, whether we can attribute the lower participation claimed by California late voters to the dissuasive influence of conclusive, as opposed to inconclusive, returns.

As a follow-up to the above series of questions, we asked specifically whether respondents, in urging others, had mentioned returns. Such allusions were naturally more frequent in California than in Ohio, where only one person answered, "Yes, [I told them] Johnson was clearly ahead." Just how the citing of returns figured in these situations is hard to evaluate, because the number who made explicit mention of them was not very large, even in California. Nor was there necessarily mention of the Johnson landslide. One reference was to indications that Goldwater seemed to be ahead; two other conversations alluded to returns from the Senate race but failed to mention the way things seemed to be going with regard to the presidency.

In a set of parallel questions, respondents were also asked whether they personally had been the targets of any such attempts to influence at any time on election day. Here the pattern was opposite that for influence attempts by the respondents toward others: More late voters in California (53 per cent) than in Ohio (39 per cent) reported that they themselves had been urged by someone to vote, or to vote for a particular person. Most of the time this meant that the respondent had been reminded to be sure to vote. We have no direct evidence to indicate whether or not this was an attempt to forestall and counteract the possible influence of returns, as mention of these was made in only a few conversations.

The nature of party organization and the tenor of political

activity differ between the two areas studied; therefore, no inference can be drawn about the possible effect of returns as a stimulus to the informal pressure to get out the vote. On the other hand, the appeal by Dean Burch of the Republican National Committee to "all of our volunteers in the Rocky Mountain and Pacific Coast states to redouble their efforts," carried by all three networks at 5:20 California time, may have received a wider hearing in the East, where polling places had closed and most people by this time had begun following returns. Significantly, only somewhat over 10 per cent of the late voters in California — compared with over 20 per cent in Ohio — cited radio or television as a source of appeals that they be sure to vote.

The most relevant difference between the two states lies in the number of persons who recalled that others had suggested that it no longer mattered whether or not the respondent himself voted. There were ten such persons in California; one person in Ohio claimed that he had been told the same thing, though this must have been before the conclusive returns began to pour in. Yet every one of these persons voted anyway. We suspect that most conversations of this nature involved the usual kind of election day banter that both contributes to and reflects the rising excitment as the day nears its end. If the race for president appeared already decided, voters would find some other reason they should vote. All these conversations helped focus attention on voting, no matter what the individual response.

We would note three additional observations on the relationship of electioneering activities in which persons were involved and their knowledge of early returns (Table 5.8). To begin with, persons with no pre-voting exposure whatsoever were least active in seeking to influence others, but were themselves slightly more often the targets of reminders that they should vote. This makes sense in terms of the two-step model of communication flow, which predicates that opinion leaders are usually more attentive to the mass-media content than those to whom this information is passed along.

In the second place, knowledge of returns, though in part a function of the higher political involvement of the party activists, may also have some independent effect. To the extent that the

Table 5.8 Conclusion Drawn from Early Returns and Electioneering Activity in California

	Conclusion Drawn							
	Johnson Certain		*Less than Certain*		*Total with Some News Before Voting*		*No News Before Voting*	
By Respondents Toward Others	N	%	N	%	N	%	N	%
Urged switch	2	2	4	4	6	3	0	—
Urged vote	26	21	35	2	61	28	15	10
By Others Toward Respondent								
Urged switch	9	7	9	9	18	8	6	4
Urged vote	49	40	40	41	89	41	68	48
Had suggested no longer vote	3	2	3	3	6	3	4	3
	(N = 123)		(N = 97)		(N = 220)		(N = 144)	

differences observed are reliable, they indicate that the person exposed to returns but not yet certain of the outcome was more likely to urge others to vote than the person who had already become certain.

Last, the few scattered dissuasion attempts were not concentrated in any way among persons who had become certain; they were, as a matter of fact, equally frequent among those who had themselves heard no early election news before they voted.

Summary of Findings

This study turned up no evidence of any last-minute shift of votes, either in favor of the indicated winner or toward the underdog. Because of the possibility that changes in both directions could have canceled one another, we took a special look at three groups potentially most open to influence by the election broadcasts:

(1) late-late voters, who cast ballots during the last ninety minutes;

(2) persons under cross-pressure, or who reportedly made some vote decision on election day;

(3) those who indicated that they had seriously considered, at one time or another, some kind of abstention from voting.

Late-late voters included an unusually large number of Republicans-in-conflict. Yet we could find no evidence either that their late appearance at the polls stemmed from a desire to first hear how the race was going, or that their overwhelming vote for Johnson had much to do with what they had heard prior to voting.

Most last-minute decisions related not to the presidency, but to the many other electoral contests held at the same time. Six out of seven crystallizations resulted in votes for Goldwater, but none of them was a direct response to what voters had heard about the presidential race.

Registered voters who during the campaign had entertained serious thoughts of not voting, or of not voting the entire ticket, were on the whole politically involved and intended their abstention as a protest against the lack of alternative advantages presented by the two candidates. (In this respect, they differ markedly from the typical late decider and nonvoter, whose political indecision is depicted in most election studies as an expression of indifference.) Pre-voting perceptions tended to reinforce their disinclination to vote. However, though they felt even less like voting after having been exposed to significant returns, the overall impact of the totality of political communications moved them to vote.

Hence the impact of the early returns on behavior was minimal. Very few examples of bandwagon and underdog effects, of either the direct or the indirect variety, were encountered. The few we were able to document had little to do with what respondents had heard about the presidential race prior to voting.

• 6 •

Certainty and Invalidation: Their Potential Impact

Does it make any difference at all that people may be certain before they go to the polls that an election is all but over? Given the law of minimal consequences (Chapter 1), one would expect few who meant to vote to be dissuaded from voting, and few who were determined to vote for one candidate to decide to vote for another. But do any of these people feel more eager or less eager to vote if they are sure who has won?

After our interviewers had ascertained just what the respondent had heard before voting and what conclusion he had drawn from this news, everyone who heard any election news was then asked: "Did what you heard make you more eager to vote in this election?" Those who answered affirmatively were invited to explain why, and those who said "no" were queried about whether it had made them "less interested in voting?" In this chapter we deal with these *direct attitudinal reactions* to what was heard.

Eagerness to Vote

There were 220 late voters in California who had heard something of how the election was going before they voted. Asked whether this news made them more, or less, eager to vote, 72 per cent reported no change in attitude (Table 6.1). Though this was obviously the typical response, there were those who

Table 6.1 Eagerness to Vote and Conclusion as to Who Would Win ("Exposed Only")

Attitudinal Reaction	*Johnson Certain*		*Johnson Probably*		*No Conclusion, Goldwater Chance*		*All Exposed to Returns*	
	N	%	N	%	N	%	N	%
More eager	27	22	5	14	5	8	37	17
Less eager	20	16	2	6	2	3	24	11
All changes (more and less eager)	47	38	7	20	7	11	61	28
No change	76	62	29	81	54	89	159	72
Total drawing conclusion	123	100	36	101*	61	100	220	100

*Due to rounding.

talked about a change in their feelings toward voting. Among this group, the "more eager" reactions outnumbered the "less eager" by approximately a 3-to-2 ratio. The net impact of hearing returns was to increase interest in voting.[1]

A close look at the 220 persons exposed to news before voting draws attention to the effect of "certainty." Some change in attitude — becoming more or less eager to vote — was more common among those who were sure of the outcome. There was a reliable difference between the proportion of those sure that Johnson would win who felt differently about voting (38 per cent), of those thinking he would probably win (20 per cent), and those who had come to no conclusion or still gave Goldwater a very good chance (11 per cent) (Table 6.1).

The data do support the common-sense assumption that the motivation to vote will decline somewhat as the outcome of the election becomes more certain. Admittedly this inference is drawn from limited evidence. It does appear, however, that the ratio of "less eager" to "more eager" reactions increases as certainty increases. Thus, the "less eager" response accounts for a

[1] Fuchs in two previously cited articles also suggests that hearing the broadcasts was more likely to increase than decrease interest in voting (*op. cit.*).

Table 6.2 Eagerness to Vote by Time of Voting ("Exposed" Only)*

Attitudinal Reaction	*Voting Time*								*Total Reaction*	
	After 4:00 P.M. But by 5:30 P.M		After 5:30 P.M. But by 6:30 P.M.		After 6:30 P.M.		Nonvoters			
	N	%	N	%	N	%	N	%	N	%
More eager	9	14	16	20	12	18	0	—	37	17
Less eager	6	9	7	9	9	14	2	29	24	11
All changes (more and less eager)	15	23	23	29	21	32	2	29	61	28
No change	49	77	59	72	45	68	5	71	158	72
Total in time period	64	100	82	101†	66	100	7	100	219	100

*Excludes one person exposed to news but on whom exact time of voting was not ascertained.
†Due to rounding.

larger proportion of all changes among those certain that Johnson would win than it does among those less than certain of the outcome.

Further, when attitude changes are ordered by time of voting, it appears that they are more frequent among those voting the latest (Table 6.2). The proportion reporting any change of attitude is not particularly large in any time period, but the "less eager" reactions increase as closing time draws near and begin to be almost as frequent as "more eager" responses. Is it possible that late-late voters and nonvoters were, to begin with, less eager to vote; that this reaction would have been more frequent however certain they were of the outcome? We checked this possibility by comparing separately the attitudinal reactions of those "certain" and those "less than certain" voting within each time period. With "certainty" so controlled, time of voting makes little difference.[2]

How much did these reactions have to do with whether a person had been following the network election coverage before he went to vote? Table 6.3 certainly reveals no striking differences in attitudinal response between those whose information came directly from these broadcasts and those who used other sources. But when we consider only those certain of the outcome before voting, we find a high proportion of "more eager" reactions among those certain of the outcome who had *not* followed the network returns. These people were apparently "eager" to reach the conclusion that Johnson had won, however scanty their information. Expecting such news, many of them were all the more "eager" to cast their ballot.

Invalidation, Bandwagon, and Underdog Effects

Chapter 3 showed that it was more difficult, and required more information, to invalidate an expectation about the outcome of

---

[2] The total number of attitudinal reactions among "certain" voters going to the polls in different time periods is remarkably similar (37 per cent, 40 per cent, and 39 per cent). Among late voters who had *not* become certain of the outcome by the time they voted, there was a slight but statistically meaningless increase in *frequency* of attitude change (12 per cent, 14 per cent, 20 per cent), but the high proportion of "more eager" reactions was maintained throughout the time periods.

Table 6.3 Eagerness to Vote and Followed Network Broadcasts of Returns of Those Certain and Not Certain ("Exposed" Only)*

Attitudinal Reaction	*Followed Network Returns Before Voting*		*Did Not Follow Network Returns Before Voting*		*Total Reaction*	
	Certain and Not Certain					
	N	%	N	%	N	%
More eager	21	16	16	18	37	17
Less eager	16	12	8	9	24	11
All changes (more and less eager)	37	28	24	27	61	28
No change	92	71	66	74	158	72
Total, certain and not certain	129	99†	90	101	219	100
	Certain Before Voting					
	N	%	N	%	N	%
More eager	14	18	13	30	27	22
Less eager	14	18	6	14	20	16
All changes (more and less eager)	28	36	19	44	47	38
No change	51	65	24	56	75	61
Total, certain	79	101	43	100	122	99
	Less Than Certain Before Voting					
	N	%	N	%	N	%
More eager	7	14	3	6	10	10
Less eager	2	4	2	4	4	4
All changes (more and less eager)	9	18	5	10	14	14
No change	41	82	42	89	83	86
Total, less than certain	50	100	47	99†	97	100

*Excludes one respondent on whom exact information on time of voting could not be ascertained.
†Due to rounding.

the election than to confirm it. Where expectations were invalidated, what was the effect of invalidation on attitudinal responses? Does "certainty" evoke a different reaction when it invalidates a prior expectation than when it serves as confirmation? Is invalidation more likely to promote a "less eager" or "more eager" response?

In 1964, where the outcome was so generally anticipated in advance, the outright invalidation of prior expectations was at a minimum. In fact, to learn something about invalidation effects, we had to categorize as "invalidation" two different pairs of expectations and pre-voting perceptions: The first consisted of an expectation that Goldwater would win or that the race would be "extremely close," coupled with a pre-voting perception that the Johnson election was either certain or at least highly probable; the second included the expectation that Johnson was the more likely winner in a fairly close contest whose outcome was far from certain, coupled with a pre-voting perception that dispelled all possible doubts. The first type of invalidation experience is no doubt more definitive than the second and more consequential, but the number of cases was too small to allow this kind of refined distinction.

The attitudinal reactions to an invalidation experience are shown in Table 6.4. As hypothesized, attitude change was more frequent when pre-election expectations were invalidated prior to

Table 6.4 Eagerness to Vote and Invalidation of Expectations ("Exposed" Only)*

Attitudinal Reaction	*Invalidation*		*No Invalidation*		*Total Reaction*	
	N	%	N	%	N	%
More eager	10	23	27	16	37	18
Less eager	10	23	14	8	24	12
All changes (more and less eager)	20	46	41	24	61	30
No change	23	53	124	75	147	71
Total exposed	43	99†	165	99†	208	101†

*Excludes twelve respondents who had heard something but on whom adequate information on other relevant items could not be obtained.
†Due to rounding.

voting than where there was no invalidation. Among those whose expectations were invalidated, 46 per cent reported some change in the desire to vote; only 24 per cent of others exposed to news before voting said they felt more, or less, eager to vote. Where the person whose expectations were invalidated reported a change in attitude, it was just as likely to be positive as negative. Among those whose expectations were confirmed, or at least not invalidated, by what they heard, positive reactions were twice as likely as negative reactions. Hence, the over-all effect of invalidation was to shift the balance of attitudinal reactions in the "less eager" direction.

Having one's expectations invalidated by pre-voting perceptions depends not only on communications exposure but also on the accuracy of one's pre-election expectations, which, as we have seen, are in turn linked with voting preferences. Partisans tend to overevaluate the strength of their own candidate. Exposed to definitive returns before voting, Goldwater supporters were thus more prone than others to experience an invalidation on election day (35 per cent among those voting for Goldwater, but only 13 per cent among Johnson voters). However, the differences in their attitudinal reactions (Table 6.5) are hardly substantial. Thirteen per cent of the Goldwater supporters felt less eager to vote, compared to 9 per cent of those voting for Johnson; 20 per cent felt "more eager," compared to 16 per cent. What over-all

Table 6.5 Eagerness to Vote and Voting Preference ("Exposed" Only)*

Attitudinal Reaction	*Voted for Goldwater*		*Voted for Johnson*		*Total Reaction*	
	N	%	N	%	N	%
More eager	16	20	20	16	36	18
Less eager	10	13	11	9	21	10
All changes (more and less eager)	26	33	31	25	57	28
No change	53	67	94	75	147	72
Total exposed	79	100	125	100	204	100

*Excludes nonvoters and respondents on whom adequate information was not obtained.

differences there were in attitudinal reactions can be attributed to the shock many Goldwaterites felt at the early returns.

Let us now construct a more refined measure of underdog-versus-bandwagon perceptions for assessing their impact on attitudes about voting. To a Johnson voter, news that Johnson had won or was clearly ahead and the likely winner was a bandwagon perception, even though he might resist drawing the obvious conclusion out of caution or superstition. To the Goldwater voter, the same news meant his man was clearly the underdog. Still, the same projective element that had led him to exaggerate Goldwater's chances might make him seize on any bit of information or surmise to sustain his hopes. We cannot, in other words, simply assume that all Goldwater supporters who heard some election news had underdog perceptions, while all Johnson supporters had clear bandwagon perceptions. Only those who drew some conclusion about the likely outcome can be classified along this dimension.

With bandwagon and underdog perceptions so defined, the following responses are noted (Table 6.6): Persons who for one reason or another did not recognize the impending (probable or certain) Johnson victory least often reported a change in their attitude toward voting (13 per cent). This proportion rose to 27 per cent among those who saw their own candidate as clearly leading, and to 40 per cent among those with underdog percep-

Table 6.6 Eagerness to Vote and Bandwagon/Underdog Perceptions ("Exposed" Only)*

Attitudinal Reactions	*Bandwagon*		*Inconclusive*		*Underdog*	
	N	%	N	%	N	%
More eager	17	17	5	9	12	23
Less eager	10	10	2	4	9	17
All changes (more and less eager)	27	27	7	13	21	40
No change	71	72	49	88	32	60
Total exposed	98	99†	56	101†	53	100

*Excludes those who refused to reveal their voting preference.
†Due to rounding.

tions. Both the "more eager" and the "less eager" reactions show parallel increases, but underdog perceptions are perhaps somewhat more potent. While they both strengthen and weaken the motivation to vote, the number of "less eager" reactions seems to increase slightly more among voters who realize that their own man has irrevocably lost.

To review our observations so far: the likelihood of a change in attitude toward voting increases as the individual (1) becomes certain of the outcome, (2) finds his expectations invalidated by returns, or (3) sees his own candidate as the underdog. The total number of attitudinal responses reported by persons exposed to *any kind* of information was 27 per cent, with "more eager" reactions representing 61 per cent of all reactions.

Let us push the analysis one step further. Certainty, invalidation, and underdog perceptions produce "more eager" reactions in just about identical proportions, in each case amounting to just under one fourth of all those with the specific type of perception (Columns 1–3, Table 6.7). The proportion experiencing a change in attitude — negative or positive — is highest among persons whose expectations have been invalidated; it is the large number of "less eager" reactions that accounts for the larger number of total reactions. Projecting from this relationship, one sees that the number of "less eager" reactions might under certain conditions actually come to exceed the more positive responses and any impetus toward voting that comes from prevoting perceptions.

What of the relative importance of the three factors — the perception that the outcome can no longer be influenced ("certainty"), the invalidation of an expectation, and an underdog perception? Which has the greatest potential for keeping voters from the polls? The first point to note is that the three categories are not mutually exclusive. For example, a Goldwater supporter who had become "certain" his candidate would win would have had both an invalidating perception and an underdog perception. Because of the way these measures were constructed, overlap between "certainty" and the other two is unavoidable. We can try to remove this methodological overlap by looking only at persons who were "certain" where this involved neither

Table 6.7 Eagerness to Vote: Comparison of Factors

Attitudinal Reaction	*Certain* (1)		*Invalidation* (2)		*Underdog* (3)		*Certain (Residual)* (4)		*Underdog (Residual)* (5)		*Certain and Invalidation* (6)		*Underdog and Invalidation* (7)	
	N	%	N	%	N	%	N	%	N	%	N	%	N	%
More eager	27	22	10	23	12	23	17	19	4	24	10	27	8	22
Less eager	20	16	10	23	9	17	12	14	1	6	8	22	8	22
All changes (more and less eager)	47	38	20	46	21	40	29	33	5	30	18	49	16	44
No change	76	62	23	53	32	60	57	66	12	71	19	51	20	56
Total, all exposed	123	100	43	99*	53	100	86	99*	17	101*	37	100	36	100

*Due to rounding.

an invalidation nor an underdog perception, giving us the "certain-residual" category (Column 4, Table 6.7). We can do the same for underdog perceptions, thereby creating an "underdog-residual" category (Column 5). It is not possible, however, to do this for invalidation, since certainty was itself an element that entered the construction of the invalidation measure.

When the effects of certainty and invalidation are removed from underdog perceptions, this causes a noticeable decrease in the proportion of attitude changes. All of the decline is accounted for by a drop in "less eager" reactions. We hypothesize that an underdog perception that does *not* invalidate expectations, but comes at a time when the outcome is *not* a foregone conclusion, has the capacity to evoke a strongly *positive* response. The number of cases is small; the differences could be chance variations, but the results are suggestive.

These comparisons also highlight the effect of invalidations when combined with either certainty or underdog perceptions. The joint effect is greater as well as more negative than the effect of either certainty or underdog perceptions alone (Columns 6 and 7, Table 6.7). An invalidation that signifies at the same time a dashing of one's hopes would appear to have a particularly strong negative potential.

We can at least suggest, though not definitively conclude, that the potential of broadcast returns to discourage voters was limited, in 1964, by the fact that invalidations were the exception rather than the rule. Our forty-three cases of invalidation account for twenty out of sixty-one attitude changes among a total of 220 exposed to pre-voting perceptions of the outcome. To the extent that for most people the election returns merely confirmed what they already expected — that Johnson would win by a landslide — one of the major hypotheses underlying our law of minimal consequences is confirmed. Had early returns invalidated expectations on a larger scale, they might have aroused a larger number of negative reactions.

One can also speculate about the potential effects of other combinations. What would have been the effect of an invalidation on a voter who had not expected his own candidate to win and then suddenly realized that there was a chance of winning, i.e., where the race was actually much more wide open than he had anticipated? In the 1964 presidential race, the typical invalidation experience was for a person to come to view his man as having definitely lost. What would be the typical response if the underdog perceptions that constituted the invalidation had been combined with perceptions that the race was still wide open, and that late voters might still influence the outcome? Such a combination — of an invalidation with underdog perceptions when the returns do not allow for definitive conclusions — could have rather higher potency.

A Test Case: The California Senate Race

In California, where balloting in certain less populated counties ended earlier than in the East Bay area, thirty-five of our late-voter sample reported, in response to a direct query, that they had heard something about the California Senate race before they went to cast their own ballot. As many as 30 per cent of those voting during the last hour before polls closed had heard such news; those voting earlier had less often heard anything and, if they had, were not very likely to draw any conclusion about who was most likely to win the Senate seat. Given the highly inconclusive nature of the scattered returns disseminated before polls closed, it is hardly surprising that twenty-one out of the thirty-five with pre-voting perceptions of the Senate race should have acknowledged that they could draw absolutely no conclusion about the probable outcome. They were evidently witnessing an extremely close race, with the few returns available showing the candidates running neck-and-neck. Explaining why they had not been able to make inferences about the probable winner, about half (10) said that the few districts in which returns had been tabulated were not representative of the entire state; the other half (11) referred to the evident closeness of the race.

Here, then, we have an instance where "certainty" can be ruled out as a major influence on reactions to returns heard. Only four of the thirty-five late voters claimed to have had this degree of pre-voting assurance from early returns. All four were early-evening voters, casting their ballots after 7:00 P.M.; one was, in fact, a last-minute voter, who had arrived at the polls just before

8:00 P.M. after hearing a projection based on computers that had made him certain Murphy would win, as he did indeed. As to the other three, we were unable to pin down what had made them so certain. There were no admissions by respondents that anyone had wrongly been "certain" that Salinger would win the Senate seat, but the ten additional late voters who drew a conclusion as to the probable winner, while being "less than certain," split evenly, four counting on Salinger and six seeing the election going to Murphy.

The ambiguous implications of these early returns notwithstanding, the responses to what was heard about the Senate race prior to voting resulted in a much higher proportion of attitude changes (48 per cent) than did the much more conclusive returns about the presidential race (28 per cent). All but one of the reactions to Senate returns represented an increase in eagerness to vote. Hence, the pattern appears quite different: A high proportion of responses is here associated with a highly positive reaction, while an increase in the number of reactions to presidential returns went with a shift in the balance toward the negative side.

Whether or not a person drew a conclusion from what he heard, exposure to Senate returns nevertheless contributed to the likelihood of some attitude change (Table 6.8). Changes in atti-

Table 6.8 Eagerness to Vote and Conclusions Drawn from Early Senate Returns ("Exposed" Only)*

Attitudinal Reaction	*Total*		*No Conclusion*		*Some Conclusion*		*Confirmation*		*Invalidation*	
	N	%	N	%	N	%	N	%	N	%
More eager	16	46	6	29	10	71	3	60	6	75
Less eager	1	3	1	5	0	—	0	—	0	—
All changes (more and less eager)	17	49	7	34	10	71	3	60	6	75
No change	18	51	14	67	4	29	2	40	2	25
Total exposed	35	100	21	101†	14	100	5	100	8	100

*One respondent with a conclusion had expected a tight race and was unable to make an estimate of the outcome before the election. Therefore the sum of those who received confirmation or invalidation is one less than the total who drew a conclusion.
†Due to rounding.

tude were reported about twice as often by persons who drew some conclusion as by persons who drew no conclusion about the probable winner from what they had heard. It did not, however, appear to matter whether the conclusions represented a confirmation or an invalidation of what the respondent had believed before the election. The response in either case was about the same, though some differences might have turned up if observations had been made on a larger sample. These data, admittedly limited, suggest that no amount of assurance about the probable winner would provide much impetus toward slack, even on the covert, attitudinal level, as long as the race remained close.[3]

The reactions to the Senate returns also provide some data for examining the relative strength of bandwagon and underdog perceptions under conditions where certainty about the outcome is evidently a minor factor. Ignoring viewers who had seen only the most incomplete returns and drew no conclusions, we can compare three groups: those reassured by bandwagon perceptions; those aware that an extremely close race was shaping up, one that could go either way; and those with underdog perceptions that showed their own man behind (Table 6.9).

Every person who drew a conclusion from returns as to the possible winner, irrespective of whether this resulted in bandwagon or underdog perceptions, reacted by becoming more eager to vote for Senator. The unusually high number of those with underdog perceptions who did become more eager again bolsters inferences, based on attitudinal reactions to presidential returns, about the greater potential power of underdog perceptions compared with bandwagon perceptions. All seven with underdog perceptions were Salinger supporters who realized that their man might lose. Seeing one's man trailing in a clearly close race led to a highly positive balance of reactions. The likelihood of a

---

[3] The figures obviously provide no justification for firm conclusions, especially since we cannot be sure how much the reports of pre-voting perceptions were contaminated by what respondents heard afterward. These few cases do not in any event support the idea that the perception of a close race constitutes an incentive toward voting, though they certainly do not refute the possibility. To this extent, then, conclusions about the impact of certainty drawn from the presidential race are confirmed by an analysis of reactions to Senate returns.

reaction to the Senate race was probably increased because the returns offered positive evidence that the race was close and that the outcome could still be affected by what late voters did.

Table 6.9 Eagerness to Vote and Bandwagon/Underdog Perceptions from Early Senate Returns ("Exposed" Only)

Attitudinal Reaction	*No Conclusion Too Early*		*Own Man Leads*		*Very Close*		*Own Man Behind*	
	N	%	N	%	N	%	N	%
More eager	3	30	4	57	3	27	6	86
Less eager	0	—	0	—	1	9	0	—
All changes (more and less eager)	3	30	4	57	4	36	6	86
No change	7	70	3	43	7	64	1	14
Total exposed	10	100	7	100	11	100	7	100

·7·

The Volatile Voters

The minimal consequences of early returns on the *behavior* of late voters is a recurrent theme throughout this book. A number of conditions generally tend to reduce the impact of mass communications. Since many of these were present on election day in 1964, large numbers of California voters flocked to the polls to carry out their vote intentions in spite of, or possibly because of, returns they had heard. Particularly striking is this finding: The proportion of late voters who became more eager to cast a ballot after hearing returns from the East exceeded those who were discouraged when they learned their vote no longer seemed to matter. Indeed, a few voters reported that early returns helped to resolve prior doubts about whether they should vote, or vote the entire ticket. Actually these crystallizations would probably have come about simply as a function of the natural climax a campaign reaches on election day, when a decision can no longer be postponed. As far as we can tell, both the turnout and the distribution of the presidential vote among our registrants were about what they would have been in the absence of early returns. We found nobody who had switched on election day, and only a single instance of demonstrated late-election-day slack.

A negative finding of this kind is hardly ever accepted as definitive. Some lingering doubt must inevitably remain — be it with regard to the selection of respondents, interviewing techniques, or the peculiar circumstances of the 1964 election. If people continued to vote as they would have, even after learning that the race for president had already been decided, there had to be some reorientation, mostly on the *covert* level, by which the apparent implications of conclusive early returns were either discounted or re-evaluated. Thus, the attitudinal reactions of voters provide clues about how consistency in behavior is maintained in the face of new circumstances.

To put this line of analysis on a firmer basis, let us first make explicit several alternate assumptions about major motivational components promoting electoral participation in the United States and other countries where voting is essentially a voluntary act. First, the pattern of attitudinal reactions can be examined on the assumption that voting constitutes primarily a *utilitarian act,* motivated by a desire to influence the outcome of an election. Second, voting has been depicted as an *expression of partisanship,* motivated by a wish to go on record as favoring a party slate, a candidate, or a policy. To the extent that this picture is accurate, electoral participation would be little affected by any decline in the utility of the vote. Third, voting represents in large measure a *testimonial of civic-mindedness* on the part of those casting ballots; it stems from a disinterested sense of obligation to participate in the electoral process. All three motives can be present at one and the same time, but responses to early returns will depend in part on which is predominant.

Voting as a Utilitarian Act

The utility of an act generally varies in accordance with two factors, the value attached to the preferred outcome and the perceived effect of one's own act in bringing that outcome about. Casting a ballot will appear to have great utility to the voter who (1) perceives considerable difference between alternative outcomes (i.e., it matters who wins), and (2) believes that his own vote can contribute to the victory of his candidate. How important these utilitarian considerations are to voters can be clarified by examining the reaction of persons whose belief in the utility of their vote was destroyed by the news that Johnson had already won.

If an election has already been decided by the time a person casts his vote, then evidently the ballot is without any practical utility. This proposition appears self-evident, and pre-election forecasts of late-election-day slack were derived from an image of voters guided by utilitarian considerations. When an election appears clearly decided, the potential influence of every additional vote approaches zero. The problem then becomes to differentiate between (1) those who saw voting as far less useful, once they heard returns, and (2) those who, to begin with, did not expect their vote to affect the result, and in any case did not care very much who won. If voting constitutes primarily a utilitarian act, the first group should exhibit the largest number of attitude changes in response to definitive returns; the motivation to vote among the second, because it must stem from considerations other than those of practical utility, should be relatively unaffected.

As regards the perception of the utility of their own vote *before* they had heard any returns, we differentiate among three clusters of late voters:

(1) the *highest utility* group, who thought that who won made a "great deal" rather than "little" difference *and* who expected their own vote to count — in the sense that they anticipated at least a fairly close race nationally and at the same time judged their own state of California, with its large block of electoral votes, to be among the doubtful states;

(2) a *moderate utility* group, who also believed their own vote would count but did *not* believe it made a "great deal" of difference who won; and

(3) a *low utility* group, who never expected their own vote to count, so that whether or not they saw much difference in the outcome is irrelevant.

It is among the highest utility group that we would expect the early returns to have most impact, but primarily among those who had become certain of the outcome before voting. Those within this same group who, though exposed to early returns, did not consider the race decided were more likely to go on believing that by voting they could still affect the outcome of the presidential race. By contrast, persons in the low utility group would have no reason to change their beliefs in response to the returns. If the perceived utility is a mainstay of the motivation to vote, the impact of knowing that Johnson had already won (or would certainly win, regardless of how the late vote went) would be greater where the vote had initially been perceived as having some utility.

We already know that attitude change occurred more frequently where early returns were interpreted to mean a sure Johnson victory, rather than just showing him ahead or the more probable winner. The question here is how much of this attitude change can be explained by changes in the perceived utility of the vote. Table 7.1 presents the evidence on attitude change among the three categories of late voters on whom we have been focusing. The first column shows the percentage difference in frequency of attitude change, regardless of direction, between those who, having heard returns before voting, were certain Johnson would win and those who did not draw such a firm con-

Table 7.1 Impact of Returns on Late Voters with Different Degrees of Perceived Utility in Casting a Ballot

Perceived Utility	*Percentage Difference in Attitude Changes Betw. Voters "Certain" and "Less Than Certain"*†	*"Less Eager" as Per Cent of All Attitude Changes*
Highest (90) Vote counts and election important	8	25
Moderate (60) Vote counts and election not so important	39	67
Low (47) Vote does not count	36	17

*This group divides into twenty-seven who thought the election important and twenty who did not. The only change of attitude among the latter was a person who became less eager to vote.

†The per cent in this column is an index of the impact of certainty on the eagerness to vote. It is calculated by subtracting the per cent of attitude changes among those with a given degree of perceived utility and who are not certain of the outcome from the percent of attitude changes among those with the same perception but certain of the outcome.

clusion. Each of these figures — 8 per cent, 39 per cent, 36 per cent — represents the *excess* of attitude changes among those certain over those less than certain.

These comparisons indicate clearly that the capacity of early returns to elicit some kind of attitude change did not depend primarily on a *change* in the perceived utility of the vote. If anything, the impact of "certainty" appears least among voters in the highest utility group. That this should be so may raise questions about positive findings on the impact of an invalidation (Chapter 6), a measure that bears a strong resemblance to the one employed here. In this connection we point out that it was the *national* outcome that was or was not invalidated, whereas in the present context the measure of perceived utility also takes account of the expected outcome in California and the definition of how important the results in that state would be. The test here is also for the incremental effect of "certainty," while the degree of certainty was itself an element in the invalidation measure.

If we now differentiate between directions of attitude change — "more" or "less" eager to vote — the importance or insignificance of utilitarian considerations in voting becomes clearer. The second column in Table 7.1 shows that a "less eager" reaction was most typical of those who had thought their vote would count but attached no great importance to the outcome of the presidential race: 67 per cent of those reporting a change in their disposition to vote felt less eager to do so. On the other hand the probability of a "less eager" reaction was not significantly different between those with highest perceived utility and those who did not think their vote would count. The suggested interpretation of all these findings is this: If changes in the perceived utility determine attitudinal reactions, this effect is most evident where involvement in the election is low and the outcome is not considered important. Involvement in the outcome is also a measure of partisanship. As such it may not only interact with, but also partly offset, the possible effect of utilitarian calculations. The possibility of such a relationship will be kept in mind during our examination of partisan involvement as an incentive to vote.

Voting as an Expression of Partisanship

Most inquiries into the social psychology of voting picture electoral participation as an expression of partisan attitudes.[1] Those with the lowest involvement in the issues that divide the electorate are apt to take the least interest in the campaign and are least likely to vote. Partisan attitudes are in part a function of pressure exerted by one's peers to choose sides and align oneself. To the extent that such attitudes are anchored in a voter's group affiliations and in his immediate social environment, electoral participation is something other than a market decision. It offers an opportunity for an ideological declaration that many voters feel impelled to make irrespective of whether or not their ballot can influence the outcome.

Furthermore, a person's vote is linked to a party symbol through which ideological positions are articulated. Partisan attitudes relate to how the public business should be conducted and to who should be in charge. The partisan through his vote seeks to mandate a certain type of government. It is through his vote that he lends his intention visible force. Even in the United States, where the ideological bases for party allegiances are not very well articulated, parties and party loyalties play a crucial role.

It should follow that voters with a strong need to put their ideological preference on record will not be readily affected by any information on the likely outcome of a contest. The assumption that voting is above all an expression of ideological partisanship can be evaluated by putting this corollary to test: Whatever is learned from broadcast returns is less likely to undermine eagerness to vote among strong partisans than among weak partisans. Certainty about the outcome should also result in more attitude change among those less partisan. Thus, returns pointing to a Johnson victory should have had relatively little effect on the strong partisan determined to lend support to and to declare his solidarity with his choice. The mere fact that an

---

[1] See S. M. Lipset *et al.*, "The Psychology of Voting," in G. Lindzey (ed.), *Handbook of Social Psychology*, Vol. II (Cambridge, Mass.: Addison-Wesley, 1954), pp. 1124–1175.

election was being held would suffice to maintain his interest in casting a ballot.

Partisanship can be indexed in a number of ways. The simplest, most direct measure is found in self-reports of respondents: A strong partisan *by such indexing* is one who believed that who won made a "great deal of difference" *and* that this election was "more important than most elections." If our hypothesis is correct, this kind of voter should have been less volatile than others in his reactions to returns heard before voting. Neither "certainty" nor exposure to less than conclusive returns should have affected his attitudinal reactions as much as those of persons with weaker partisan commitments. Similarly, any changes among strong partisans should have been predominantly in the "more eager" direction.

Comparisons shown in Table 7.2 permit a test of both expectations. The arrangement follows the logic already used in Table 7.1, with the first column of figures representing the percentage

Table 7.2 Impact of Returns on Late Voters with Different Degrees of Partisan Involvement in the Election

Involvement	*Percentage Difference in Attitude Changes Betw. Voters "Certain" and "Less Than Certain"**	*"Less Eager" as Per Cent of All Attitude Changes*
Strong partisans (self-reported)	(+) 19	(+) 20
Weak partisans (self-reported)	34	70
Nonchangers during campaign	(+) 17	(+) 26
Waverers and switchers	37	54
Straight-ticket voters	24	(+) 31
Split-ticket voters	19	70
Consistent voters (1960–64)	25	(+) 28
Floaters (1960–64)	21	59
Party-oriented	(−) 35	(+) 31
Candidate-oriented	19	42
Mean difference	+2	+32

(NOTE: All differences in the amount of attitude change favored those "certain." A plus sign indicates a difference of over 10 points in the direction of support for the hypothesis; a minus sign, a difference of over 10 points in a direction contrary to the hypothesis.)

*See note to Table 7.1.

difference in the amount of attitude change between those certain of the outcome as a result of hearing returns, and those not yet able to draw so certain a conclusion. The second column indicates the proportion of "less eager" responses. Plus or minus signs prefixed to some pairs of percentages indicate differences between strong and weak partisans sufficient to either support (+) or contradict (—) the expectations.

When we compare strong and weak partisans, as identified by their self-reports, it appears that partisanship has some inhibitory effect on volatility. Not only does certainty have greater impact on weak partisans, but their attitude changes represent mainly a decline in eagerness to vote.

The degree of partisanship can also be indexed by evidence of consistency and stability in voting preferences. Such a measure permits the effect of partisan involvement to be tested by comparing attitudinal responses of:

(1) persons who had a consistent preference throughout the 1964 campaign, and those who had been wavering in their support for one of the candidates or were in doubt on whether they should vote at all;

(2) straight-ticket voters, and those who either split their vote or abstained from voting for one or both of the major offices;

(3) those who voted for the 1960 and 1964 presidential candidate of the same party, and "floaters," who went from the candidate of one party to the candidate of another; and

(4) voters whose preference was principally a choice between the parties, and those who were mainly guided by the characteristics of the candidates.

In each case, the group whose preferences were consistent over time and anchored to a party image should be, according to the hypothesis, less volatile in their reactions.

The pattern of responses gives some indication of the complexity of the relationships involved. We now have five measures of partisan involvement. When two are used — self-reports and changes during the campaign — certainty has a greater influence on the amount of attitude change among weak partisans than among strong partisans. When the other three are used, the difference is in the opposite direction; but, except for the comparison between "party-oriented" and "candidate-oriented," it is quite small. When the five comparisons are averaged, the mean difference of attitude change between strong and weak partisans is only two percentage points. The hypothesis that certainty will have significantly less effect upon strong partisans is not confirmed.

On the other hand, the predominant response of the strong partisan — however identified — was to become more eager to vote. Weak partisans contributed quite disproportionately to the total number of "less eager" reactions (Second column, Table 7.2). Indeed, except for those defined as weak partisans because they are candidate-oriented, the majority of weak partisans reacted to election news by feeling less inclined to vote. Apparently partisanship had a determinate influence on the direction of those attitudinal changes that did occur, but not on the incremental effect attributable to "certainty."

Specific political factors that differ from election to election always confound the relationship between partisanship and the process by which people arrive at an electoral decision. The 1964 election may not have signified a permanent political realignment of the American electorate, but there is no doubt about the large number of Republican defections in response to Goldwater's highly controversial candidacy. Of the 32 per cent within the California sample identified as "floaters," the overwhelming majority were Republican defectors. Repelled by the Goldwater brand of Republicanism, they cast their votes for Johnson. Many were voting against a candidate; many split their tickets between Johnson and Murphy, and a disproportionate number wavered in their decisions and considered abstaining. None of these acts in themselves imply a lack of ideological commitment or a view of the election as unimportant; yet, each is an index of comparatively low partisan involvement. Thus a number of Republicans who normally might show up as strong partisans were in 1964 weak in their party commitments.

One politically significant grouping consists of sixty-six registered Republicans whose primary ballots were cast for Rockefeller. Their participation in the primary, when turnout was much lower, testifies to at least some degree of political involvement. Yet this group contributes disproportionately to deviations from normal party voting. Of these sixty-six Rockefeller voters, forty cast a presidential ballot for Johnson; only twenty-four remained loyal to their party by voting for Goldwater, with the remaining two refusing to reveal how they had voted. One third of this group voted a split ticket. The reason they wavered and had difficulty in arriving at a firm decision belies somewhat the picture of the volatile voter[2] as a person neither politically involved nor motivated by political considerations.

To pin down the relationship between partisanship and motivation to vote, the attitudinal reactions of these pro-Rockefeller Republicans were compared with those of Republicans who had supported Goldwater in the primary and those of still other registered Republicans who failed to cast a primary ballot (Table 7.3). The pro-Rockefeller Republicans, although subject to political cross-pressures, exhibited the least attitude change in re-

Table 7.3 Eagerness to Vote by Vote in Republican Primary ("Exposed" Only)*

Attitudinal Reaction	*Goldwater*		*Rockefeller*		*Did Not Vote*	
More eager	9	27	3	8	2	10
Less eager	2	6	1	3	3	14
All changes (more and less eager)	11	33	4	11	5	24
No change	22	67	34	89	16	76
All exposed	33	100	38	100	21	100

*Includes only registered Republicans.

[2] V. O. Key, *The Responsible Electorate; Rationality in Presidential Voting, 1936–1960* (Cambridge, Mass.: The Belknap Press, 1966). Ch. 2 makes the same point on the basis of rather different data.

sponse to returns. The loyal Goldwaterites exhibited the largest amount of attitude change, but most of it was a reaffirmation of their previous intention to vote. If there is a concentration of "less eager" reactions, it appears to be among persons not sufficiently involved to have cast a primary ballot.

The small cell frequencies make any firm conclusions impossible. Yet they appear to underline the previous observation that responses were to a considerable extent independent of the perceived utility of the vote. The dissuasive influence of returns was most evident among persons whose involvement was low to begin with, whereas Goldwater Republicans more typically became more eager to exercise their franchise, even if the returns told them of a certain Johnson victory. The ideological commitment of many to the Goldwater brand of Republicanism suggests a shift of attention away from victory and toward the margin of the majority.

By a shift of attention many with strong partisan involvement can sustain the motivation to vote. Thus, the perceived utility of casting a ballot does not depend solely on its capacity to influence the contest for a single office, even if that office is, as it was in this case, the presidency of the United States. By shifting his interest and concern to other issues and races that are not nearly so focal, the partisan can maintain his belief in the utility of voting. Such a shift was evident among some regular Democrats, who worried that news of Johnson's sweep might cause slack and so jeopardize Salinger's chances. Awareness of this possibility made them more eager to vote. Similarly, there were a few Republicans in conflict over whether to vote their party or their convictions who, once they learned their presidential ballot could no longer affect the outcome, turned their exclusive attention toward ensuring victory for Murphy, hoping thereby to counterbalance the painful defeat in the contest for the highest office.

None of the news of the Senate race heard before voting permitted any certain conclusion, except that the race would be close. This evident closeness increased the eagerness to vote among a rather high proportion of those who had heard Senate returns. The number of such attitudinal reactions elicited by these inconclusive returns far exceeds that from among persons who had defined the presidential returns as inconclusive. Hence, we wondered how many positive motivational responses to the Johnson landslide reflected judgments about its effect on the outcome of the senatorial contest in California. After all, had not press reports and campaign statements just before election day expressly alerted the public not to stay home in the event of an early unambiguous indication of a Johnson victory? Partisan attitudes that extended to the Salinger–Murphy contest would become focal as the presidential race began to appear decided. They would bolster the motivation to vote even after the ballot could no longer affect the outcome of the race for the highest office.

This displacement of motivation, whereby certainty of presidential victory might make partisans more eager to vote lest Salinger be defeated, would be greatest, we reasoned, among two categories of persons: (1) those who expected the Senate vote to be so close that the result could easily be overturned if even a small number of voters stayed home; and (2) those who had been alerted to the possible effect slack caused by news of the Johnson victory might have on the senate race. Most of the latter were Democrats voting for Salinger. No direct questions were asked about this. In inquiring directly into such matters one always runs the risk of planting in the minds of respondents ideas not previously harbored; the interpretation can only be checked out indirectly.

First, attitudinal reactions to presidential returns were cross-tabulated with prior expectations concerning the California Senate race (Table 7.4). The net increase in eagerness to vote was greatest among those expecting an extremely close contest between Murphy and Salinger. Twenty-five per cent of these persons became more eager to cast a ballot as a result of hearing returns from the presidential race. This contrasts sharply with the reactions of persons who evidently had expected Salinger to be swept into office by the Democratic tide. Among this group, certainty of a Johnson victory elicited an unusually large amount of attitude change, sixteen out of thirty persons, with eleven persons reporting they felt less like voting upon learning that John-

Table 7.4 Effect of Certainty on Eagerness to Vote* by Respondents with Different Expectations of the Senate Outcome

	Expectation of Senate Outcome															
	Extremely Close				*Republican Winner*				*Democratic Winner*				*Don't Know*			
Attitudinal Reaction	*Certain*		*Less Than Certain*		*Certain*		*Less Than Certain*		*Certain*		*Less Than Certain*		*Certain*		*Less Than Certain*	
	N	%	N	%	N	%	N	%	N	%	N	%	N	%	N	%
More eager	17	25	3	7	4	21	2	11	5	17	4	17	1	14	1	11
Less eager	6	9	2	4	3	16	1	5	11	37	1	4	0	—	0	—
All changes (more and less eager)	23	34	5	11	7	37	3	16	16	53	5	21	1	14	1	11
No change	44	66	40	89	12	63	16	86	14	47	19	89	6	86	8	89
Total exposed	67	100	45	100	19	100	19	100	30	100	24	100	7	100	9	100

*Answers to: "Did what you heard [about the presidency] make you more eager to vote in this election? . . ."

son had definitely won. Even those who emphatically denied that conclusive presidential returns affected their eagerness to vote occasionally supported these disclaimers with an explanation that they still wanted to vote for senator, for the other offices, or for some of the propositions. Thus, becoming less eager to vote could only imply a relative lack of concern about the effect of slack on the outcome of other contests, particularly of the California Senate race.

When we examine separately the reactions of Murphy and Salinger voters to presidential returns, clear differences in net reactions turn up. Persons who voted for Murphy had become "more eager" and "less eager" in just about equal numbers, but among Salinger's supporters the net response was strongly in the "more eager" direction (Table 7.5). No such difference, it will be recalled, was observed between the reactions of Goldwater and Johnson voters to presidential returns.

Before the significance of this observation can be interpreted, it is necessary to control statistically for the impact of invalidation; as noted earlier, having one's expectations upset promotes a distinct decrease in the eagerness to vote. When the senate vote is cross-tabulated with whether the results were an invalidation, the increase in "more eager" reactions is shown to be most characteristic of Salinger supporters who had counted on a Johnson landslide all along. Coached beforehand about the possible effect of any late-election-day slack on Salinger's chances for reelection, very few of them became less enthusiastic about voting. There is no hint that attitudinal responses of Murphy voters were influenced by invalidating perceptions based on early returns.

This phenomenon, whereby a shift in concern toward the fortunes of the candidate running for the lesser office helps maintain the margin of the candidate running for the higher office, represents a *reverse coat-tail effect.* The plurality for Johnson, who had already won and no longer needed any additional votes, must have been partly sustained by voters going to the polls because of their concern with Salinger's chances. We believe that a reverse coat-tail effect played some role, though a subordinate role, in inhibiting slack among California late voters. Appar-

Table 7.5 The Effect of Invalidation on Eagerness to Vote Among Salinger and Murphy Voters*

Attitudinal Reaction	*Voted for Salinger*						*Voted for Murphy*					
	Invalidation		*No Invalidation*		*Total*		*Invalidation*		*No Invalidation*		*Total*	
	N	%	N	%	N	%	N	%	N	%	N	%
More eager	4	40	16	20	20	22	6	19	10	14	16	16
Less eager	3	30	3	4	6	7	6	19	9	13	15	15
All changes (more and less eager)	7	70	19	24	26	29	12	38	19	27	31	31
No change	3	30	61	76	64	71	19	61	52	73	71	70
Total exposed	10	100	80	100	90	100	31	99†	71	100	102	101†

*Nonvoters and abstainers from Senate race are excluded, as well as those for whom adequate information was not available.
†Due to rounding.

ently, regular Democrats were most likely to follow this pattern. Their perception of the utility of their votes was preserved by partisan commitments that extended to races other than the main attraction. It survived even the "election" of the president. Republican stalwarts, by contrast, appear to have been more strongly motivated by ideological involvements, by a wish to go on record regardless of what the presidential returns showed.

Voting as a Civic Obligation

Casting a ballot also expresses a more basic and permanent orientation to the electoral process, one that is to a degree independent of both the desire to influence the outcome and partisan (ideological) involvement. Many, perhaps most, Americans grow up with the idea that voting for president is a sacred duty. Their positive attitude toward the responsibilities of citizenship develop long before they have specific perceptions of who the officeholders are and the functions they perform, or of the parties and what each stands for.[3] A person's sense of obligation to cast a ballot as an expression of his civic-mindedness prevails even when the vote appears to have no purpose, as in an uncontested election or in one that offers the voters a choice between Tweedledee and Tweedledum. Consequently the proportions among various population groups who vote in a presidential election reflect the prevalence of this general attitude. It is not very much affected by either the closeness of the race or the specific issues at stake.

The point is that the vote, whatever else it may also express, represents a kind of testimonial, with some characteristics of a symbolic act. Positive attitudes toward participation in the electoral process are in fact so ingrained among registered voters that many cast ballots simply and primarily so as not to appear derelict in their citizen obligations. *Not* voting would require a deliberate decision on their part. This nonrational commitment to voting can likewise be observed in an election where the outcome appears a foregone conclusion, as it did in 1964 to many

---

[3] Fred I. Greenstein, *Children and Politics* (New Haven, Conn.: Yale University Press, 1965).

Californians who had heard conclusive returns by the time they went to the polls.

Among general attitude clusters related to the likelihood that a person will vote are a *sense of political efficacy* (confidence in one's ability to influence the political process), and a *sense of citizen duty* (a conception of civic responsibility). According to the University of Michigan Survey Research Center, voters in a national election exhibit these attitudes to a more marked degree than those who fail to vote.[4] A third attitude cluster related to voting participation is *alienation from politics.* Alienation is similar in some respects to a low sense of political efficacy, but it also reflects the tenuousness of the motives that underlie the political participation of a certain type of voter. The alienated voter is mobilized primarily in those elections that present a suitable focus for hostile feelings, so that the ballot is employed as a form of sanction.[5]

As a measure of political efficacy, we used three test statements from a scale developed by the Survey Research Center group. The respondent could either agree or disagree that:

> "People like me don't have any say about what the government does."
>
> "So many people vote in elections that it rarely matters whether one votes or not."
>
> "Sometimes politics and government seem so complicated that a person like me can't really understand what's going on."

All three statements elicited such a high measure of disagreement among our sample of *registered* voters – both in California and Ohio – that only persons disagreeing with *all three* were rated as "high" on political confidence. By this criterion 46 per cent of the voters in California exhibited high political confidence. The other 54 per cent were judged to be "low" because they did not measure up to this optimum.

---

[4] A. Campbell *et al., The Voter Decides* (New York: Harper and Row, 1954).

[5] M. B. Levin, *The Alienated Voter: Politics in Boston* (New York: Holt, Rinehart and Winston, 1960).

Agreement with another statement borrowed from the Michigan Center — "Voting is the *only way* in which a person like me can influence government officials."—measured, for our purposes, a strong *commitment to voting.* A slight majority disagreed, presumably because they believed in the existence of other ways, like writing to one's congressman, working through a pressure group, or picketing the White House. Still, the conception of voting as the "only way" probably indicates a stronger and less qualified view of the efficacy of the ballot and the obligation of the respondent to exercise his franchise, regardless.

Voters were also asked, "When you voted for president, would you say you were voting more *for* one of the candidates, or *against* one of the candidates?" Nonvoters were asked how they evaluated the relative merits of the two candidates. They were given the choice among "both pretty good," "one definitely better than the other," and "neither particularly good." In each instance, negative responses were taken as indicative of *alienation.* About two out of five voters said that their vote was primarily a vote "against." Thus, attitudes of hostility against the alternatives available in this election were fairly widely diffused. We do not imply that this attitude in every instance reflected a generalized sense of alienation, but many voters evidently felt far from enthusiastic about the alternatives between which they were to choose.

The three attitudes obviously overlap. Low confidence in one's ability to affect governmental policy assigns low utility to the ballot and weakens the sense of obligation to vote. The significance of voting as the "only way" is ambiguous; the alienated may see voting in these terms, since he has no faith in other ways of exerting influence on government, yet this same response by another person may reflect a very positive attitude, a belief in the importance of the ballot as the "only way" in which the mass of citizens are assured of attention to their views by officeholders.

The assumption was that registered voters who were *low* in political confidence, *not* committed to voting as the "only way," and *alienated* (insofar as they were voting "against") would be more volatile. Accordingly, we expected those among them who had been certain at the time they went to the polls that Johnson had won to register more attitude changes than those not yet certain, and that all of them would be especially prone to have "less eager" reactions. Table 7.6 indicates that these attitude items were related to volatility, but not so consistently as our reasoning led us to suppose. Both those low in political confidence and those who were voting "against" a candidate reacted comparatively strongly to returns indicating the election was all but over. Certainty, on the other hand, appears to have had a *slightly* greater impact on those seeing voting as the "only way," but the difference is, in any event, small.

Once again the basic attitudes of voters seem to have had more influence on the direction of the response than on the likelihood of a response. Political confidence, low alienation, and a high sense of civic obligation made people more eager to vote even when it seemed to make little difference in the outcome.

Casting a ballot represents for many voters something akin to a sacred duty, one in which they do not care to be remiss. In the words of one respondent, "voting is a God-given right." In this respect, then, a voter's desire to exercise his franchise has some of the elements of an expressive gesture through which he signifies his belief in the electoral process as a meaningful and viable

Table 7.6 Impact of Returns on Late Voters with Different Degrees of Political Confidence, Citizen Obligation, and Alienation from Politics

	*Percentage Difference in Attitude Changes Betw. Voters "Certain" and "Less Than Certain"**	*"Less Eager" as Per Cent of All Attitude Changes*
Political confidence — high	17	29
	(+)	
Political confidence — low	29	43
Vote "only way"	28	27
"Other ways"	22	58
Voted "for" a candidate	16	30
	(+)	
Voted "against" a candidate	39	54

*See Table 7.1 and, for explanation of + sign, Table 7.2.

procedure for conducting the business of the nation. The legitimacy this process enjoys supports other attitudes that in turn help support the motivation to vote. Were early returns pointing toward a clearly one-sided race to undermine the belief in the efficacy of the electoral process, this could in the long run change the pattern of voting turnout.

Bandwagon Philosophy

The nonrational desire to vote in an election is consistent with a yearning many people have to be in the mainstream of a new political movement or, more generally, to see themselves in step with the times. This is, in fact, the basis for the widespread belief in a bandwagon effect. Many people project on to others their own wish to be on the winning side. Accordingly, they assume that the man who appears to be ahead and by a large majority will attract a significant number of additional votes.

Data on election-day decisions and on the attitudinal reactions of Johnson and Goldwater voters provide no evidence of any significant bandwagon effect resulting from returns people heard before voting. If there was any such influence, it was either too subtle or affected too few votes to turn up in the course of this study. A brief examination of these beliefs, and of the attitudes that support them, may nevertheless be instructive.

To begin with, more than a third of the late-voter sample agreed with the test statement that "Public-opinion polls hurt the chances of the candidate they say is behind." Asked whether they thought the pre-election polls might have influenced the outcome of the 1964 election, some 40 per cent stated either that they certainly had or that this was at least highly probable. Invited to spell out what these alleged influences were, nearly all of these respondents referred in one turn of phrase or another to bandwagon effects. Still, all of these respondents failed when it came to documenting bandwagon effects with anecdotal accounts either about themselves or about anyone else they personally knew.

We also encountered much spontaneously voiced criticism of the broadcasting of returns before polls everywhere had closed. The criticisms were most frequently directed at computer projections from incomplete returns, and although they were somewhat less explicit in their reference to bandwagon effects, nevertheless reiterated in other respects tenets of the demonology that has become familiar with regard to pre-election polls. Some typical and far-from-extreme quotes are:

"The returns should not be announced until polls are closed in California."

"I believe that polls throughout the country should open and close all at the same time."

"Computer predictions greatly affect voters in the Far West who are undecided."

"I dislike it when they predict. I think it can influence people out here."

"People might like to be on the winning side."

To repeat, these same people who believed in bandwagon effects from polls and broadcasts denied being guided in the least by the bandwagon philosophy in their own behavior.

All late voters were asked to agree or disagree with two additional test statements incorporating two tenets of this philosophy: "If I have no clear preference, I like to be for the man who is running ahead," and "If you vote for a loser you are wasting your vote." The first of these two statements elicited agreement from only 4 per cent of the late voters in California — and from 8 per cent in Ohio. The second statement was accepted as correct by even fewer: only 2 per cent in both states. This similarity in the distribution of responses makes it unlikely that they were influenced to any great degree by unique experiences California late voters underwent on election day. Yet, guided by their belief in the dire influences of predictions, some California late voters went out of their way to avoid contamination. Here is how one of them described the way he had quarantined himself against their potential influence: "I purposely had not listened before I went to vote. . . . I wanted to think [for myself]."

The post-election reassertion of a belief in the potent effects of the bandwagon contains at least an element of rationalization, a search for scapegoats on whom to blame defeat. Thus, the belief in the operation of poll effects was found to have been most widespread among Goldwater voters, who remained steadfast in their vote, the apparent Johnson landslide notwithstanding. Whereas 51 per cent of Goldwater voters thought that the polls had contributed to the defeat of their man, only slightly over 30 per cent among those voting for Johnson were willing to entertain this viewpoint.

The political demonology draws strength from another quarter — from a distrust of the ability of social science to predict behavior, including the outcome of an election. This distrust is, moreover, consistent with low political confidence and feelings of alienation, as well as with a conservative political ideology that defines social events as outside the realm of intelligent control. Thus Goldwater supporters coupled their dismay at the outcome with diffuse criticisms of the use of computers. "Prophesying robots" was the way one person referred to them. "It gives you a feeling of defeat," said another, "of 'what's-the-use-anyway'." Not surprisingly, then, one finds a comparatively lower level of belief in the operation of polling effects among persons who had voted for the winner, and an even lower figure (by one percentage point) among those who had voted for Salinger, the Democratic senator who attributed to the early election coverage part of the blame for his defeat.

The difference between Republicans and Democrats could also be a function of what each cared to remember of Truman's unexpected victory in 1948, which for a time discredited the pollsters. However, the more important point is that voters have by now become highly aware of the possibility of poll effects and act, individually as well as collectively, to counter them in advance. In spite of or because of this, the widely current belief in bandwagon effects does not accord with the actuality. The majority of those who, upon hearing returns, became certain of the outcome felt no different about voting than they had before, and the changes that occurred among the rest could not be attributed in any way to an endeavor to ride with the bandwagon.

There are in fact good reasons for discounting bandwagon effects as a likely reaction to early election returns. In the first place, the effect of a majority in persuading deviants to fall in line is greatly reduced when it speaks with less than a unanimous voice.[6] Even the lopsided majorities Johnson amassed amounted to less than two thirds of the votes cast, a majority too small to have yielded the familiar laboratory effects. Second, within the various groups that together constitute the electorate, there occurs something during the campaign more or less akin to a bandwagon: Specific groups become politically more homogeneous as individual deviants go with the majority. In the third place, the entire electorate serves as a reference group guiding behavior in only a most general way. To the extent that it does, its norms tend to legitimate party conflicts. Finally, after the election is over and the loser has conceded, every effort is made to reestablish the semblance of national unity. In contrast to what takes place in a political convention, the legitimacy of the opposing party is thereby reaffirmed.

Considering the institutional context within which voting takes place, there is no reason to believe in the existence of bandwagon effects in direct response to what appears to be a majority. The volatile members of the electorate seem not to be especially responsive to such influences, and their voting participation, in any event, lacks firm roots. The majority among the registered voters, the vast mass of the electorate, for reasons discussed above, will simply not be affected.

---

[6] S. E. Asch, "Effects of Group Pressure upon the Modification and Distortion of Judgments," in E. E. Maccoby *et al.* (eds.), *Readings in Social Psychology*, 3rd ed. (New York: Holt, Rinehart & Winston, 1958), pp. 174–183.

8

The Late Vote: Summary of Findings and Their Implications

The reporting of the 1964 national election made communications history. For the first time there was the chance that conclusive returns, including projections of the final outcome, would be available to many voters in Western states before they themselves had voted. While networks had used computers to "pick winners" as early as 1952, such machines, fascinating as they were to broadcasters and audiences alike, had remained a novelty or sensation not to be taken too seriously. By 1964 computer application in this area had reached a new stage of sophistication, and the networks and press associations decided to pool resources to provide the public with the fastest possible tally of results. The new technology combined with the collaborative effort held a clear prospect that the networks would be able to point to significant trends indicated by bellwether precincts within minutes — and certainly within the hour — after voting ended at 6:30 P.M. in several strategic Eastern states.

Citizens throughout the country, but especially in California, were forewarned of possible political effects in the event the networks announced a probable winner early on election night. Newspaper editors and columnists, radio and television commentators, and others voiced their active concern. Political managers and their candidates took to the air and called press conferences urging those who might vote late not to be dissuaded by whatever they might hear.

Some of these warnings raised the specter of vote shifts as returns began coming in. There were allusions to bandwagon effects benefiting the man shown to be ahead, as well as talk of a large sympathy vote for the apparent underdog. These were not, however, the chief concern. The great expectation was that, were early returns to show Johnson with a decisive lead in the East, a drop in Western voter turnout could have a determinate influence on the outcome of the election. People who would otherwise have gone to the polls might be led to think that their votes no longer mattered, and in particular those who had already experienced some disinclination to vote might be discouraged from going to the polls. Finally, there was concern over the number who might put off voting until they could first check the returns. These persons would also be open to dissuasive influences.

Events on election day 1964 clearly corroborated the expectation of an early declaration of the winner from very incomplete returns, long before the polls in California had closed. In the precincts studied, three out of five registered voters who had not yet gone to the polls by 4:00 P.M. local time had heard something about how the race for president was going by the time they voted, or, in the case of nonvoters, before the polls had closed. Over half of these (or one out of three persons interviewed) were able to conclude from what they had heard that a Johnson victory was certain and that the race for president had, for all practical purposes, already been decided. Only six persons (less than 2 per cent of the sample) had heard some returns that left them with the impression that Goldwater was making a comparatively strong showing.

The two broadcast media were, beyond doubt, the chief source of these pre-voting perceptions; they were mentioned as the primary source of information by 81 per cent of those who had been exposed to election news by the time they voted. More people mentioned radio than television, probably because many tuned in as they drove home from work or to the polls. Yet television was clearly the more effective in apprising viewers of the outcome. This effectiveness does not appear to be so much an attribute of the medium as of media use. In contrast to radio listening, television viewing was more likely to occur after work, when the returns coming in were more definitive and viewers could give them more attention. The network coverage provided a fairly clear indication of the impending Johnson victory from the minute it went on the air: 71 per cent of those who followed these returns from 4:00 P.M. on said that, as soon as they turned on their set, they knew "right away" that the race was more or less decided. This proportion increased to near 90 per cent among persons who first tuned in at a later hour. The 15 per cent who received what information they got before voting from other people were probably hearing second-hand what originally came over radio or television.

It must nevertheless be emphasized that not all the information with which California late voters went to the polls, nor the conclusion they drew, came from the early network election coverage, which had begun at 4:00 P.M. local time and had made full use of computer-based projections. Even in Cleveland, where these network broadcasts did not begin until after polls had closed, one out of seven late voters and nonvoters interviewed claimed that he had heard something of how the election was going while he could still make a vote decision, and a few said that they had become certain of the impending Johnson landslide. Consequently, one can assume that even if the network election coverage had been delayed until polls everywhere had closed, Californians voting late would still have had more information about election trends before they voted than late voters in the East. This is because polls in the East Bay area closed four and a half hours later than in Ohio, and news bulletins on local stations could carry reports of voting trends from other sections of the country.

Most people indicated that they drew their conclusions about the probable outcome *not* from computer predictions but from tallies of the popular vote and of the electoral vote shown by the networks. Yet the 16 per cent who did base their conclusion on computer reports were more often certain that Johnson would win by the time they voted. These persons were better informed both about what computers could do and about politics. The latter characteristic, by itself, might account for why they were able to draw this conclusion earlier than others.

Interest in an early prediction appears to have been stronger among late voters in Ohio, where 25 per cent chose this as one of their reasons for selecting a particular channel, than in California, where this reason was chosen by only 11 per cent. Apparently Easteners wanted to know the outcome of an election without having to stay up most of the night, whereas Californians could count on hearing significant results by poll closing time. Yet sizeable minorities both in California (45 per cent) and in Ohio (38 per cent) agreed with the statement that "being told who the winner will be early in the evening before most votes have actually been counted takes the fun out of election-night broadcasts."

The conclusion a person drew from returns available did not depend solely on these reports, but also on what he had expected beforehand. It obviously took more information to invalidate an expectation that Goldwater would win than to confirm one about a Johnson landslide. Those who had anticipated a landslide became certain of the outcome prior to voting about twice as often as those who had given Goldwater a chance — in a close race or otherwise. Political preference, by contrast, made little difference: Goldwater supporters were as likely as Johnson supporters to accept the fact of a Johnson victory.

The Broadcasts and Voter Turnout

How much late-election-day slack can be traced to the special network broadcasts? Our interviews with 364 Californians, all of them registered, supplemented by an effort to account for 339 other nonvoters whose names appeared on precinct rosters, paid off in one single case of late-election-day slack in response to the broadcasts: an angry Goldwater supporter, who said he had never given Goldwater much chance but was so dismayed by the lopsided Johnson margin that he simply gave up and did not vote.

A single case hardly provides a sound basis for quantitative generalization. As a further check we therefore compared the nonvoting rate within our thirty-three California precincts with that in the nine comparable Ohio precincts, using for this purpose the official tabulations of the vote. Our investigation disclosed the dangers inherent in deducing effects from differences in rates between the two areas. Approximately two thirds of so-called nonvoting in the precincts in both these states was due to failure to remove from voting rosters the names of voters who had died or moved to another district; thus these official nonvoting rates reflect a good deal of residential mobility and mortality. After the appropriate corrections had been made, the actual amount of nonvoting among registered voters in California turned out to be a mere 4 per cent instead of 13 per cent. This figure of 4 per cent represents the upper limit of the range within which broadcast-induced late-election-day slack could possibly have occurred. This is to say, if *every* registrant who did not vote had heard network returns before polls closed and had thereby been dissuaded from casting a vote, a maximum of 4 per cent of the electorate could have been so affected.

The California nonvoting rate of 4 per cent was actually lower than the rate in Ohio, where it amounted to 7 per cent. Much of the verified nonvoting in both states was due either to illness, or to the unavoidable and unanticipated necessity to be out of town. Hence this logical — but obviously improbable — upper limit must be further reduced by at least the number who were physically unable to vote. Among those remaining — perhaps 2.5 per cent of all registered voters — lack of political interest was clearly the most important reason for failure to appear at the polls.

When we focused specifically on the impact of network broadcasts, their subordinate importance as a cause of slack became still clearer. To begin with, a smaller proportion of nonvoters than late voters had been following returns before polls closed. Nonvoters as a group had clearly less interest and were less involved in the election campaign. Since both these characteristics — interest and involvement — would lead a person to follow network election returns before voting and stay with them until the early hours of the morning, long after all doubts about the outcome had been dispelled, the relatively lower exposure of nonvoters gains further credence.

As far as those who voted are concerned, the time a person went to the polls seems to have had more influence on the time he started following returns than vice versa. Though late voters who cast ballots during the last ninety minutes of voting more often had been following returns by that time, or heard at least something about election trends, than those voting earlier, we failed to locate a single person who had deliberately delayed his vote until he could first learn how things were going. Rather than seeking politically useful information, those who had watched before voting did so for the spectacle the returns normally offer or simply out of habit, absorbing whatever is on the air.

Vote Decisions

We also investigated the alternative possibility, namely that the election broadcasts may have encouraged vote switching or helped crystallize the votes of persons who had serious doubts about whether they should vote and whom to vote for. Long before the interview turned to the broadcasts, we asked all late voters whether they had made any vote decision on election day itself.

Most decisions mentioned by respondents related to their votes on candidates for lower offices or for a proposition. An identical 2 per cent in California and Ohio reported a decision affecting their vote for president. None of these decisions involved a switch. Rather they were crystallizations — i.e., decisions to vote by people who had thought about abstaining. The number of crystallizations in Ohio, obviously, cannot be attributed to the election broadcasts, but neither could we establish any cause-effect relationship between the returns and the decisions made by the California late voters. In fact, the crystallizers had less often heard returns before voting and were less likely to have become certain than those who merely followed through on decisions made before election day.

The process of vote crystallization can also be viewed in its temporal sequence. We asked each voter whether he had ever "seriously considered," at *any time* during the campaign or on election day itself, any one of these three alternatives: (1) not voting at all; (2) voting without casting a ballot for president; or (3) voting without casting a ballot for U.S. senator. We found that of the twenty-four voters who had played with the first alternative, every one ultimately voted. Indicative of the central role played by the presidential contest in getting out the vote is that only three of the thirty-seven persons who had considered not voting for president actually cast a ballot without pulling the lever for the highest office; among the persons who had entertained this alternative with regard to voting for United States senator, a much larger proportion (six out of twenty-one) actually abstained. Again the pattern was similar in California and Ohio, providing no indication that the returns played any significant part in this regard.

Attitudinal Reactions

Analysis of reactions went beyond the impact of the broadcasts on votes to the more general issue of why people should continue to cast ballots for president after it had become evident that the outcome could not possibly be overturned. We had collected data meant to get at people's covert and attitudinal responses to what they heard and saw. From these reports about how they felt, one can gain some insight into how they might react under circumstances when these tendencies pass over the threshold from covert responses to overt behavior.

Asked whether election information had made them more eager or less eager to vote, the large majority (72 per cent) of those who had heard returns while they could still make a vote decision said that it had made no difference at all. Among the others, the number who became more eager to vote outnumbers those who became less eager by a 3 to 2 ratio. The likelihood that there would be a change of attitude, and the direction it would take, depended in part on the perceptions of voters and on what these perceptions implied about the outcome of the race.

To begin with, the attitude changes follow a fairly persistent pattern: the larger the proportion within any category to report a change, the more "less eager" reactions there were relative to the number of "more eager" reactions. Thus, persons who had become certain of the outcome experienced more attitude change, and more of them felt less like voting, than persons who had not drawn such definite conclusions from the returns. In other words, as more complete returns began coming in, their unambiguous implications began to persuade a larger number of the futility of casting a vote. Yet there were many others who, this apparent futility notwithstanding, became even more determined to vote. Similarly, there were more changes among those whose expectations were invalidated by the information of the Johnson landslide, and again this was accompanied by a disproportionate increase in the number of "less eager" reactions. Indeed, the impact of "certainty" on feelings about voting depended in large measure on whether a person had become certain of a previously-held expectation or whether he had been definitely proved wrong. Finally, if certainty about the outcome involved at the same time an underdog perception, some demoralization occurred, but there were also a good many others all the more determined to have their ballots counted.

In the California Senate race, however, the very scattered and partial returns available to a few by the time they went to vote resulted in a much more definite increase in eagerness than did the conclusive presidential returns. The largest number of "more eager" reactions came from Salinger supporters who saw their man was trailing. Slight underdog perceptions, coming at a time when the outcome of that contest was still very much in doubt, appeared to have a definite mobilizing effect.

Some statements volunteered by late voters about their perceptions of the presidential race indicate that concern over the outcome of the senatorial contest may in fact have helped forestall any tendency toward slack. Salinger voters became distinctly "more eager" to vote after hearing that Johnson had definitely won than did those who were voting for Murphy. Especially prone to this reaction were Salinger voters who thought the Senate contest would be extremely close. By contrast, those confident their favorite would win were more inclined to react to news that the presidential contest was over, if they reacted at all, by becoming less eager to vote.

The Law of Minimal Consequences

Why was the effect of the returns on the behavior of voters so minimal? In explanation, we point to factors and conditions, some general and some specific to the 1964 election, that inhibited the potential of the election broadcasts to elicit behavior disjunctive with prior voting intentions. The fact that very few such specific consequences could be observed in the short run does not, of course, preclude the possibility of quantitatively and qualitatively more important effects in other elections or over the long run.

Attenuation of any impact returns could have had comes from (1) the smallness of the group potentially open to influences, (2) the neutralization of any impetus toward change by countervailing influences, and (3) the stability of attitudes that support voting and the different specific cognitions with which these attitudes are compatible.

• *The susceptible group* — To be susceptible to any influence on election day, a person has to be registered in advance, defer voting until after significant returns have begun to come in, tune in on the election coverage or talk with someone who has, and then find the image on which his vote intention is based invalidated. Mere confirmation from returns heard before voting of what a person already believes in the offing is unlikely to cause him to deviate from prior intentions.

According to best estimates, some two thirds of all California citizens of voting age were registered in 1964. Between 25 and 30 per cent on the lists from which the California sample was drawn had not voted by 4:00 P.M. local time. Some of these turned out to have moved or died. Fewer than half had been following network election returns prior to voting though about three-fifths had heard at least some election news. The percentage of registrants thus susceptible to direct influence from broadcast news was certainly no higher than fifteen per cent, and probably much lower. Among the exposed group, chances that returns would invalidate expectations were low; most respondents had never expected anything but a Johnson victory by at least a comfortable margin.

One is moreover led to expect, on theoretical grounds, that those persons most open to influence by broadcast returns are those least interested in the campaign and with the least partisan involvement. Yet many of these persons, because they do not register, are also beyond the range of possible influence from the returns. Nor was there any evidence that voters who showed up to vote during the last ninety minutes were an exceptionally volatile group, one that was disinterested in the election and pushed into voting only by a last-minute electioneering drive. On the contrary, this group of late-late voters included a rather larger number of politically sophisticated "independents," conflict-ridden as far as the 1964 election was concerned but not especially prone to rush on the bandwagon or cast a sympathy vote for the underdog. Since their concern extended to races other than that for the top office, casting a vote still made sense even after the presidential race appeared irrevocably decided.

The less politically interested, involved, and sophisticated a person, the smaller was the chance that he had heard something about the race or had been following network returns before he voted. These same characteristics were also associated with a person's ability to make an accurate assessment of Goldwater's chances before the election. Hence, a large proportion of people whose expectations could have been invalidated were exposed to returns either only casually or not at all. That the election returns should have provided a shock for so few people implies that whatever bandwagon or underdog psychology was at work must already have had its effect on people prior to election day.

• *Countervailing influences* — The influence of returns reaching voters on election day might be offset by other communications to which they were being exposed. Among these were the urgings to Goldwaterites that they vote early to avoid the possibility of influence, and the warning Salinger issued to his followers not to be lulled into complacency by an apparent

Democratic tide. At the same time, the nonpartisan saturation campaign to get out the vote continued right through election day and inundated voters from every side.

Many respondents reported that they themselves, on election day, had urged others to be sure to vote or had themselves been so urged by others. Reports of partisan attempts to switch votes by political argument were far fewer in number. Only twelve persons — all of whom voted — indicated either that they themselves had been the target of a suggestion that it no longer made much difference whether or not they voted, or that they had voiced this feeling to others. While all of these manifest dissuasion attempts were made with reference to election trends, it is at least highly probable that they nevertheless helped focalize attention on the election, contributed to the excitement, and emphasized that voting was the order of business for this day.

• *The motivation to vote* — We identified three different orientations, all of which to some extent enter into the subjective significance of casting a ballot. The reactions of voters to returns will differ in accordance with which of these orientations is dominant. Thus, the common-sense expectation that news of a Johnson landslide would cause slack was predicated on an image of the voter as motivated primarily by the utility of his ballot, by whether it could influence the outcome. This type of voter would be dissuaded from casting a ballot once the election appeared decided and his ballot could no longer affect the outcome.

A voter's partisan involvement, the second of the orientations, contributes to the stability of reactions in the situation just described. Where the vote serves primarily as an ideological expression, as a declaration of solidarity, it is to that extent independent of practical political considerations; it has a strongly symbolic character. Moreover, when perceived within a context of partisan involvement, the belief that one's vote has utility can be maintained even after one or the other candidate appears clearly to have won. The partisan perspective helped some voters to assess the implications of the presidential returns for the outcome of other races and for future elections. Some became more eager to vote because of their concern over the possible effect of the news about the presidential race on the outcome of the Senate election in California. Still others wanted to hold down the Johnson margin, or to repudiate the Goldwater brand of Republicanism so unambiguously that it would cease being a political force to be reckoned with. In these various respects, a person's vote decision differs from a market decision. The partisan label, in giving consistency to a number of preferences, converts the vote into an expression of ideology.

Stability in electoral participation is further supported by a third orientation, one that neither takes account of the utility of the vote nor has anything to do with partisanship. The nonrational commitment to voting as an obligation of citizenship implies that the vote also serves as a testimonial of faith in democratic government. Not all who continued to cast ballots, especially those who became more eager to vote after hearing conclusive returns, were guided by a political logic. A confidence in the ballot as an effective instrument for influencing government policy gave their votes the character of a ratifying gesture. This type of commitment to voting, when widespread, is an indication of the legitimacy the electoral system enjoys among the electorate and, at the same time, is one of its main supports.

Implications

The findings just summarized document the degree to which the short-run effect traceable to the early broadcasting of returns in the 1964 election conformed to the law of minimal consequences. But this law, as we have pointed out, represents only a probability statement, one that applies to direct effects in the short run. Given the novelty, in 1964, of the early declaration of a presidential winner, the question naturally arises as to how much one can possibly generalize about future elections from a case study of a single election held in a unique historical context. Another question concerns the possible existence of other, more subtle effects operating over the long haul, namely such side effects as a result from attempts on the part of individuals and institutions to adapt themselves to similar contingencies in the future.

Impact in Other Elections

The impact of early returns was shown to depend on four sets of factors: the content of *pre-voting perceptions* and how widely they are disseminated, *prior estimates* among the electorate as to the probable outcome, the *electoral choices* voters are being asked to make, and the characteristics of the *electorate*. The first of these is clearly the most variable, but any effect that these perceptions will have is mediated through the other three factors.

Returns that provide an unambiguous picture seem to have a greater impact on attitudes than returns whose significance is difficult to assay. Thus, late voters who had become certain of a Johnson victory were more likely than others to feel "more eager" or "less eager" to vote. That this should be so is, of course, highly plausible. The unambiguous character of the information reduces the opportunity to maintain by means of selective perception such beliefs as one prefers, or to preserve one's hopes by refusing to draw any conclusion at all. Characteristically, persons exposed to returns they judged to be inconclusive reported the least amount of attitude change in response to what they had heard. Ambiguity can, however, have two sources. The first is *the broadcasts themselves,* as when returns are just beginning to trickle in, when the projection shows the man with the fewer votes to be the likely winner, or when there is a contradiction in the predictions of two networks. Or, second, the ambiguity derives from a *race too close* for predictions to be made with any confidence. The analysis of the reactions of persons who drew different conclusions from these presidential returns does not, by itself, permit any inference about whether the two types of ambiguity will have the same or different effects.

In the California Senate race, we have an instance where the returns were, to be sure, altogether inconclusive, but where all the portents pointed to an unusually close race not likely to be decided early in the evening. These returns elicited an extremely high proportion of attitude changes from those exposed to them — almost all represented an increase in eagerness to vote.

It would seem, from our various findings, that returns that give an unambiguous indication of a close contest have the strongest mobilizing influence; a "decided" race apparently creates some tendency toward slack, though this was, as we have seen, partly inhibited by other factors. Returns that are confusing or open to a wide range of interpretations apparently have the least impact one way or the other. Consequently, the earlier a network can confidently predict the outcome from even a small proportion of the vote, and the more predictions of this sort find acceptance, the greater the potential demoralization of late voters as a result. On the other hand, the longer the drama of seesaw battle can be maintained, the more will the excitement so generated facilitate voting. In 1964, the effect of early presidential returns and of news of the Senate race worked in opposite directions.

The meaning of inconclusive returns was closely linked to what a respondent had been led to expect by pre-election forecasts. To a person counting on a Johnson landslide, returns that contained no indication of victory could only mean that more votes had still to be counted; to a person primed to expect a "cliff-hanger" between Salinger and Murphy, even the first inconclusive returns were apt to serve as a reaffirmation. The point is that early returns have greater impact when they serve to invalidate what has been expected in advance.

Not only were there few instances of clear-cut invalidation in 1964, but the likelihood of an unusual number occurring in future elections is greatly reduced by the growing acceptance of pre-election forecasts based on scientific polls. Improvement in these techniques and the wider dissemination of the results contribute to a uniformity of expectations, based as they are on identical sources of information. The self-appointed expert with his ear close to the ground is disappearing, and the projective element in popular estimates is likewise on the wane.

Many respondents voiced their belief that pre-election polls had influenced the outcome in 1964. Whatever the validity of charges that the polls, by presenting Goldwater as the underdog, adversely affected his chances their influence on reactions to the election broadcasts cannot be denied. Because the forecasts of a completely one-sided race were so fully confirmed even by the earliest returns, they helped immunize voters against the possibility of an invalidation. Only if polls should undergo another fiasco, comparable to the one in 1948, will returns upset the expectations of many voters.

Finally, there is at least some suggestion that underdog perceptions have a stronger mobilizing effect than bandwagon perceptions. Even if the absolute magnitude of this effect is small, a combination of invalidation and underdog perceptions in what is proving to be a close race could have a definite influence on the outcome. Some partisans in particular would become more eager to vote. Under these circumstances, the mobilization of only a minuscule percentage of the electorate could overturn the result.

The likelihood of such an eventuality is very much reduced in an election where voter interest is widely dispersed among many electoral contests instead of being focused on a single race or referendum. Our data clearly indicate that slack can be inhibited by concurrent balloting for other offices, contests in which the outcome still hung very much in doubt even after the presidential race had been fully decided. Accordingly, all other things being equal, one predicts that the danger of slack is greatest in areas of one-party dominance (inasmuch as the outcome of other races is unlikely to be affected by any falling-off in the vote for president), in party primaries where the contest is only for a single office, in special by-elections, or in a referendum called to resolve some particular issue.

The above-mentioned types of contests have in common still another feature, namely a lower and generally more variable turnout rate. The efficacy of the last-minute effort to bring out the vote, as well as the possibility of slack, are increased to the extent that there are marginally-committed registered voters, who may decide to vote or not to vote in response to highly variable social-psychological influences. The electorate in a national election evidently does not have this character. Those who vote are strongly committed toward voting, and most nonvoting, as we have seen, results from institutional and physical obstacles in the way of a 100-per-cent turnout. However, the easing of registration requirements or the institutionalization of some administrative procedure whereby registration would become "automatic" could swell the number of registered voters only marginally committed to voting in a national election, and so contribute to potential instability.

Long-Range and Ancillary Effects

Any innovation in communications — the admission of the press to legislative debates, the broadcasting of political party conventions, the televising of presidential press conferences, etc. — has invariably evoked alarm. Some change always accompanies such innovation, but the potential danger to political institutions is, in retrospect, almost always found to have been exaggerated. The process by which individuals react and the ramifications of their reactions for the workings of institutions is always more complex, and hence the effects far more subtle, than the alarmists can anticipate. Indeed, the high-pitched sense of alarm may itself be one of the firmest guarantees against sudden disjunctive change.

Long-term adaptation to the fast count and computer-based predictions involves learning how to live with them. For the individual voter, this means learning to evaluate the meaning of any apparent trend or explicit prediction. Will repeated experience with computer-dominated election night reports increase, or decrease, any susceptibility to influence? The answer depends on many things, including whether trust in the returns (and their accuracy) grows or declines; the amount of critical reserve among the audience; the tendency to vote early or to avoid pre-voting exposure to returns.

To begin with, the accuracy of early electoral trends and predictions will have something to do with the credibility they will enjoy. Performance so far has been pretty mixed. It has already been mentioned that in 1960 one network first called the election for Richard Nixon, though this prediction was quickly modified as soon as sizeable returns began to come in. Again, in the June California primary preceding the 1964 election, an early prediction by pollster Lou Harris, vividly remembered by many voters there, nearly rebounded to the discredit of the network concerned. The narrow margin by which the prediction was vindicated in the final returns helped feed the subsequent controversy over broadcast-induced effects.

Past mistakes have evidently made broadcasters more cautious. They have become increasingly careful to explain the basis on which predictions are made and to hedge their predictions with semantic qualifications — "probable winners," "indicated winners," "declared winners," etc. In some state and local elections since 1964, first predictions had to be rescinded. Yet there was little embarrassment or public outcry. The broadcasters had made allowance for such possibilities from the start of their programs.

As broadcasters gain experience in living with computers, and viewers, too, become more experienced, trust in predictions appears to grow as well. The more experienced among the election night audience, we found, were not only more knowledgeable about how predictions are made long before all votes are in, but also had more faith in the accuracy of the predictions. Not everything about these predictions was new; elections have almost always been called before the official vote count was completed. It would seem likely that as more voters come to understand the distinction between the tally of the vote and the projection of trends from sample districts, more will also recognize that broadcasters are simply applying a new technology to improve their interpretations of trends in the returns.

If trust in the reliability of the fast returns is likely to increase with their increasing accuracy, there is still the question of whether voters will also increasingly act to avoid possible influence. There is by now an acute awareness among voters in Western states that they constitute special targets of influence. This awareness, bound to increase, coupled with the exercise of responsible caution by broadcasters, should minimize the amount of influence on voting behavior by exposure to incomplete returns. Beyond this, if broadcasts continue to begin before polls are closed, individuals and groups will act consciously or unconsciously to avoid influence, and will adapt to the speed-up in returns. People obviously can deliberately vote before returns become available; they can avoid hearing news; they can persuade themselves in advance of the importance of the margin of victory or of the other races.

Still, the general inference from this and other studies — that the net balance of changes in votes had no effect on the outcome of the election in 1964 — does not mean that the broadcast of returns before polls closed had no effects upon voters or that there will not be effects in the future. While interviewees indicated that they had not changed their intention to vote (or not to vote) as a result of their exposure to news before voting, many did feel that casting a vote knowing the election was over amounted to a partial disenfranchisement. Their ballots seemed to count less.

Even when knowing the likely outcome before voting does not contribute to such feelings of alienation, it can make it more difficult to vote out of simple sense of obligation. It is altogether possible that in the future, in areas where early returns are available long before polls close, voters will learn to estimate the utility of their vote before voting. Imagine, for instance, a very close election where early returns indicate that California — or Oregon, or Hawaii, or Alaska — would supply the electoral votes necessary for victory. With the electoral votes in other states already accounted for, attention would turn to the West and what voters there would do. If the expectation of a close race had been widespread and if many people were undecided about whether to vote or for whom to vote, large numbers of people might delay going to the polls until they had first heard how the election was going. The fact that few voters waited around in 1964 does not mean that more might not do so in some future election.

Conceivably, having a good idea of how the race was going could, under some circumstances, alter the general tendency not to vote for a third party in presidential elections. The necessity, under a two-party system, for electoral coalitions presents a formidable barrier in the way of third-party protest. People who feel they are voting for the lesser of two evils are especially disinclined to defect to a minor party for fear of bringing the real evil to power. Early returns may give them a better knowledge of the odds. There is in this not so much the possibility that an election would be won or lost as a result, but that new considerations might enter the electoral choice. Instead of registering their preference between viable choices, voters would be encouraged to use what information they had from polls and returns to make their vote decisions in terms of a rational strategy.

Again, most outcry against the early returns centered on the disenfranchisement of the late Western voter. However, the time could come when those in states voting after returns were coming in are looked upon as unfairly advantaged. Any information that enables a person to see the consequence of his vote can be seen as giving him an advantage over others not so favorably situated. It is precisely to reduce disparities in access to knowledge that the press has insisted on unrestricted publicity.

In no sense, however, does this re-create the situation of a town meeting, where the roll is called and where everyone can see how the vote is about to go. Here persons can "pass" in order to cast their vote at a more crucial time; they can, for that matter, reverse their vote if, given the existing division, they come to find it advisable to do so. In a national election, by contrast, a ballot is irrevocably cast. Although the individual ballots are secret, those voting late have more opportunity to base their own vote on estimates of political trends. They may be the only ones to vote knowing that a decision has already been made. To carry this argument one step further: The canons of courtesy have generally enjoined a loser to concede—even long before the tally has been completed—as soon as the trend is unmistakeable. Theoretically a candidate could concede even while balloting was still in progress. What would the voter do then?

Clearly all the above, though logically tenable, are not likely to occur in fact. In raising these possibilities we do mean to indicate that the way election returns are reported is an important part of political life in the United States. Alteration of the election night ritual is bound, over the long run, to have consequences for political behavior. To stay up on election night to learn who the new president will be has been, especially since the advent of radio, an opportunity to participate in a national event. Election night has been a unifying experience containing elements of the "sacred." To a query about whether the fun had gone out of election night, a near-majority of Californians responded by saying the experience was not the same. When, in addition, issues are raised about how many votes were changed or races determined as a consequence of the broadcasts, the returns become linked to the divisive controversies that any electoral campaign inevitably arouses.

Technological innovations, by their nature, call for new sets of rules to cope with their effects. Certainly the new technology for data processing and quick dissemination makes it possible to have more reliable forecasts within shorter spans of time. Predictions of winners are bound to come sooner and sooner after polls close. Many voters have a keen interest in learning the outcome of an election as soon as this information becomes available, and competition among the news media will make voluntary restraints difficult to enforce. Even were early returns to be banned all over the country until polls were closed, it would be difficult to keep information from private reports — campaign managers, partisans, etc. — from leaking out. The normal flow of news would not cease, but there would be less check on its reliability. Surely, a full coverage by a professionally competent and responsible staff is preferable to news leaks designed to advance partisan interests. Any measure that curtailed the right of news-gathering agencies to check up on returns, or to disseminate them to some areas, would indeed represent an interference with the right of the public to know.

The proposal, publicly proposed by Dr. Frank Stanton, for a uniform polling day with balloting all over the country ending at the same hour, would permit the fullest exploitation of the new technology. Results from all parts of the country would be available at about the same time, so all suspicion that early returns might affect the outcome of any given race would be eliminated. Indeed, there would be no "early returns". After all polls had closed, the quick answers provided could contribute to a feeling that people all over the country were sharing in a simultaneous experience. The fun and excitement of the long vigil into election night would be abbreviated, but it would no doubt be replaced by a new ritual of interpretation-in-depth of the returns (what groups and sections voted what way), and a new ritual of concession and victory statements. Perhaps more attention would be given to state and local contests.

The justification for new election regulations does not reside in the demonstration of direct effects: Actual changes in voting behavior were few in number though various types of voters felt either more eager or less eager to vote. But given the power inherent in the new communication technology, setting rules to maintain equality seems preferable to depending on self-immunization by individual voters, or to trusting that politicians will employ strategies to neutralize the advantage one or the other side might enjoy. It is the long-range and ancillary effects of broadcasting early returns before polls close with which social policy must be equally concerned.

Index

A B C D E F G H I J 5 4 3 2 1 7 0 6 9 8